CORPORATE FINANCE FOR BEGINNERS

How Non-Finance Professionals Understand Money, Valuation, and How Companies Really Make Money

ANGELITA RODRIGUEZ B

Disclaimer

This book is provided for **educational and informational purposes only**.

It is **not** intended as financial, investment, accounting, legal, or tax advice. The author is not acting as a licensed financial advisor, investment advisor, or accountant. While every effort has been made to ensure accuracy, financial concepts and regulations may change over time, and individual situations vary.

Before making any financial, investment, or business decisions, you should consult with a **qualified professional** who understands your specific circumstances.

This book is an **independent educational guide**, created to help beginners understand corporate finance concepts clearly and confidently.

This publication is independently published.

About the Author

The author is a corporate finance educator and writer with over **15 years of experience** teaching finance to **non-finance professionals**, entrepreneurs, MBA students, and early-career managers.

With a background spanning corporate finance advisory, financial analysis, and business education, the author has worked with companies across multiple industries, helping leaders understand **how money actually moves through a business**, and how better financial decisions create long-term value.

Rather than focusing on complex formulas or academic theory, the author specializes in **clear, jargon-free explanations**, real-world examples, and practical intuition. This approach has helped thousands of readers and students overcome their fear of finance and gain the confidence to read financial statements, evaluate business decisions, and think like owners, not just employees.

This book was written for people who never planned to become finance experts, but still need to understand money to succeed.

Preface

Why This Book Was Written

Most people work with money every day, yet very few truly understand it.

Budgets are approved, reports are shared, numbers are discussed in meetings, big decisions are made. And still, many smart, capable people quietly feel lost when the conversation turns to finance.

If that sounds familiar, you are not alone.

For years, corporate finance has been presented as something only accountants, bankers, or CFOs can understand. Thick textbooks. Heavy formulas. Complex language. All of it makes finance feel distant, intimidating, and unnecessary for "regular" professionals.

But here is the truth.

Corporate finance is not about complex math. It is about understanding how businesses survive, grow, and sometimes fail.

It is about knowing:

- Why a company can be profitable and still run out of cash
- Why growing sales does not always mean growing value
- Why some businesses attract investors while others struggle
- Why certain decisions look good on paper but hurt in real life

Every manager, entrepreneur, employee, and professional is affected by these ideas, whether they realize it or not.

This book was written for people who never planned to study finance, but still need to understand it to make better decisions at work and in business.

You do not need a finance background to read this book.
You do not need to love numbers.
You do not need to memorize formulas.

What you need is clarity.

In these pages, corporate finance is explained the way it should have been explained from the beginning.

Step by step. In plain language. With real examples that make sense in the real world.

By the end of this book, you will be able to read financial statements without fear. You will understand the difference between profit and cash. You will see how pricing, hiring, expansion, and funding decisions affect a company's future. You will understand what a business is really worth and why that value changes.

Most importantly, you will stop seeing finance as something distant and technical.

You will start seeing it as what it truly is.

A practical way to understand how businesses make money and how good decisions are made.

This book is not here to turn you into an accountant or a financial analyst.

It is here to help you think clearly, ask better questions, and make smarter choices with confidence.

That is what corporate finance is really about.

And that is what this book is here to teach you.

PART I
FOUNDATIONS: HOW BUSINESSES AND MONEY WORK

CHAPTER 1
What Corporate Finance Really Is

Most people hear the word finance and immediately think of complex math, confusing formulas, or people staring at spreadsheets all day.

That reaction is understandable. Finance has not always been explained kindly.

But corporate finance, at its core, is much simpler and far more practical than most people realize. It is not about memorizing formulas or becoming an accountant. It is about understanding how businesses make decisions with money.

This chapter lays the foundation for the entire book. If you understand this chapter well, everything else that follows will feel logical instead of overwhelming.

What Corporate Finance Means in Simple Terms

Corporate finance is the study of how companies use money to achieve their goals.

That is the simplest and most accurate definition.

At its heart, corporate finance answers very practical questions such as:

- Where should the company spend its money?
- How should the company get the money it needs?
- How can the company grow without running out of cash?

Think of corporate finance as the money decision system of a business.

A simple analogy helps.

Imagine a household. A family earns income, pays bills, saves for the future, borrows when necessary, and decides how to spend money wisely. A business does the same thing, just on a larger scale and with higher stakes.

Corporate finance is simply how a company earns money, spends money, manages risk, and plans for the future.

The key difference is this: companies must do these things not just to survive, but to create value for owners and investors over time.

It is also important to understand what corporate finance is not.

Corporate finance is not just accounting. It is not just budgeting. It is not just investing in stocks. It is not just number crunching.

Those areas are related, but corporate finance focuses on decisions. It asks one central question again and again: **Is this a good use of money or a bad one?**

Once you see corporate finance through that lens, it becomes far less intimidating.

Corporate Finance vs Accounting vs Personal Finance

One reason many beginners struggle with corporate finance is because it is often confused with other financial fields. Let's separate them clearly.

Corporate finance focuses on how businesses make decisions with money. It deals mainly with planning, evaluating options, and choosing the best path.

Examples of corporate finance questions include:

- Should the company invest in a new factory?

- Should it borrow money or raise new ownership capital?
- Should it expand into a new market?
- Is this business worth buying or investing in?

Accounting, on the other hand, focuses on recording what has already happened. Accountants track revenue earned, expenses incurred, assets owned, and liabilities owed. Accounting tells you what happened last month or last year.

A useful way to think about it is this: accounting is the rear-view mirror, while corporate finance is the steering wheel. Both are important, but they serve very different purposes.

Personal finance is another separate area. It deals with individual money decisions such as saving for retirement, managing personal debt, budgeting household expenses, and investing personal savings.

While some concepts overlap, the goals are different. Personal finance focuses on personal security and lifestyle. Corporate finance focuses on business survival, growth, and value creation.

This distinction matters because approaching corporate finance with the wrong mindset leads to poor decisions. Businesses cannot make emotional or purely personal money choices. They must think in terms of risk, return, and long-term value.

Why Corporate Finance Is About Decisions, Not Math

This may be the most important idea in the entire book.

Corporate finance is not about math. It is about judgment.

Yes, numbers are involved. But numbers are tools, not the goal.

Many people fear finance because they believe they must be good at math or memorize complex formulas. In reality, most real-world finance decisions are not made by calculators alone.

They are made by people asking questions such as:

- Does this decision make sense?
- What could go wrong?
- Is the risk worth the reward?
- Can the company survive if things do not go as planned?

Those are thinking questions, not math questions.

Imagine a company considering opening a new store. The numbers may show expected sales, estimated costs, and projected profit. But the numbers cannot tell you how competitors will react, whether customer behavior will change, or whether management can execute the plan effectively.

Corporate finance uses numbers to support decisions, not to replace thinking.

At the beginner level, most corporate finance relies on simple math: basic arithmetic, percentages, and comparisons. The real challenge is learning how to interpret numbers and connect them to real business decisions.

That is why this book focuses on intuition first and calculations second.

Who Needs Corporate Finance Knowledge and Why

Many people assume corporate finance is only for finance professionals. That assumption is costly.

Entrepreneurs need corporate finance to avoid running out of cash, price products correctly, decide when to grow and when to slow down, and understand what their business is truly worth. Many businesses fail not because the idea was bad, but because financial decisions were poor.

Managers and team leaders also need corporate finance. Every time a manager approves a budget, hires new staff, expands a department, or chooses between suppliers, a financial decision is being made. Without financial understanding, managers rely on instinct alone. With it, they make informed choices that protect the company.

Employees and professionals benefit as well. Understanding corporate finance helps you understand company performance, see why leadership makes certain decisions, communicate better with executives, and position yourself as a valuable contributor. Professionals who understand finance often advance faster because they speak the language of decision-makers.

Investors and analysts rely heavily on corporate finance to evaluate companies, assess risk, and understand value. Even if you never become an investor, understanding how investors think gives you powerful insight into how businesses are judged.

How Finance Drives Business Success and Failure

Every business decision has a financial impact, whether it is obvious or not. Corporate finance sits at the center of those decisions.

Companies that succeed financially tend to manage cash carefully, invest wisely, avoid excessive debt, understand their costs, and focus on long-term value rather than short-term appearances. These outcomes are not accidental. They are the result of good financial thinking.

On the other hand, many business failures are caused not by bad products, but by poor financial decisions. Common causes include growing too fast without cash support, taking on too much debt, ignoring costs, misreading financial statements, and chasing revenue instead of profitability.

In many cases, the warning signs were visible in the numbers, but leadership did not understand them.

Consider two companies selling the same product. One grows slowly, manages cash carefully, and reinvests profits wisely. The other grows aggressively, borrows heavily, and ignores cash flow.

At first, the aggressive company looks more successful because sales are higher. Over time, it struggles to pay bills, service debt, and survive downturns. The careful company survives and eventually wins.

That difference is corporate finance.

Key Takeaways

- Corporate finance is about how businesses make decisions with money.
- It focuses on future choices, not just past records.
- Corporate finance is different from accounting and personal finance.
- The subject is about judgment and thinking, not complex math.
- Entrepreneurs, managers, employees, and investors all benefit from understanding it.
- Good financial decisions drive long-term business success.
- Poor financial decisions are a leading cause of business failure.

You now have the foundation. From this point forward, every concept you learn will connect back to one central idea: corporate finance exists to help businesses make better decisions with money.

CHAPTER 2

How Companies Really Make Money

Many people think they understand how companies make money. After all, we see sales figures, advertisements, and store openings all the time.

But here's the truth: **making money in business is not as simple as selling a product or service**. A company can sell millions of items and still be in trouble. Understanding how money really moves in a business is the foundation of corporate finance.

This chapter will help you see beyond the surface. You will understand **revenue, costs, profit, business models, and cash flow**, and why high sales do not always equal success.

Revenue, Costs, and Profit Explained Clearly

At the most basic level, a company makes money through three key pieces: **revenue, costs, and profit**.

Revenue is all the money the company brings in from selling goods or services. Think of it like the total amount of money you earn at your job before paying bills.

Costs are what it takes to run the business. These include:

- **Fixed costs** – costs that stay the same no matter what, like rent or salaries
- **Variable costs** – costs that grow with business activity, like raw materials or packaging

Profit is what's left after subtracting costs from revenue. But here's where it gets tricky: **profit on paper is not always the same as cash in the bank**. A company can show profit but struggle to pay bills if money hasn't yet come in from customers or if too much was spent upfront.

Example: Imagine you sell custom t-shirts. You sell 100 shirts at $20 each. Your revenue is $2,000. But the t-shirts cost $10 each to produce, and you also have a $500 monthly rent for your workspace. Your costs are $1,500 ($1,000 for shirts + $500 rent). Your profit is $500.

Looks good, right? But if customers haven't paid yet, or you bought extra shirts upfront, you might not have $500 in cash to spend.

The key lesson: revenue minus costs equals profit, but **profit is just a snapshot of financial performance, not always a guarantee of cash in hand.**

Why High Sales Do Not Guarantee Success

Many beginners assume that if a company is selling a lot, it must be thriving. Unfortunately, that is not always the case.

High sales can mask serious problems:

- **High costs** – If it costs more to make or deliver a product than the money it brings in, the business loses money even with huge sales.
- **Cash flow issues** – Customers may pay late, or suppliers may demand cash upfront. You could be profitable on paper but still struggle to pay employees or rent.
- **Debt and financial obligations** – Borrowing to fund growth can create financial pressure that high sales alone cannot relieve.

Example:
A restaurant may have $1 million in yearly sales. But if it spends $900,000 on food, staff, rent, and debt repayment, the profit is only $100,000. On top of that, if rent increases or a supplier demands upfront payment, the business could be in trouble despite the impressive sales figure.

This is why **finance-savvy entrepreneurs never look at revenue alone**. They also examine costs, cash flow, and financial obligations.

Understanding Business Models and Cash Generation

Not all businesses generate money the same way. Understanding **business models** is crucial to seeing how companies really make money.

Some common business models:

1. **Product-based** – The company sells physical items (like electronics, food, or clothing). Cash comes in when products are sold. Profit depends on controlling production costs and pricing correctly.
2. **Service-based** – Money comes from providing expertise or labor (like consulting, hairdressing,

or cleaning). Costs include staff time, training, and tools.

3. **Subscription-based** – Customers pay regularly for ongoing access (like Netflix or gym memberships). Revenue is predictable, but the company must retain subscribers.
4. **Platform or marketplace** – The company connects buyers and sellers (like Uber or Airbnb) and earns a fee or commission. Cash flow depends on transaction volume and fees collected.

Each model has unique risks and cash patterns. A subscription model may look small in sales at first but generate reliable cash over time. A product business may have spikes of revenue but also unpredictable costs. Understanding this is key to evaluating any company.

The Flow of Money Through a Company

To understand corporate finance, it's helpful to visualize how money flows in a business.

1. **Money comes in** – Revenue from customers.
2. **Money goes out** – Costs to operate the business, including staff, rent, materials, marketing, and debt payments.

3. **Profit remains** – The "leftover" after costs. This can be reinvested, saved, or paid to owners/shareholders.

Think of a business as a water tank:

- Revenue is water coming in through a pipe.
- Costs are holes and pipes letting water flow out.
- Profit is the water that stays in the tank for later use.

If inflow is greater than outflow, the tank fills. If outflow exceeds inflow, the tank drains, no matter how impressive the inflow appears.

Example:
A small bakery may make $10,000 in sales one month. But it spends $4,000 on ingredients, $3,000 on staff, and $2,500 on rent and utilities. That leaves only $500 in profit. Even though the sales are strong, the cash left to invest in expansion is small.

Understanding the flow of money in a company is critical. It shows why businesses can fail even when sales are high and why cash management is often more important than revenue growth.

Key Takeaways

- Revenue is the total money a company earns; costs are what it takes to operate; profit is revenue minus costs.
- High sales do not guarantee success. Profitability and cash flow are what really matter.
- Different business models generate money differently, and understanding the model is key to evaluating a company.
- Money flows in, goes out to cover costs, and profit is what remains. Mismanagement of any stage can harm the business.
- A company's health cannot be judged by sales alone; understanding cash and cost structure is essential.

CHAPTER 3

The Three Core Financial Decisions Every Company Makes

Every company, no matter its size, industry, or location, faces **three core financial decisions**. These are the pillars of corporate finance.

Understanding them is like learning the basic controls of a car before you start driving. Once you grasp these three decisions, the rest of corporate finance begins to make sense naturally.

These three decisions are:

1. **Investment decisions** – Where should money be spent?
2. **Financing decisions** – Where does the money come from?
3. **Payout decisions** – What happens to the profits?

All three are deeply connected. Poor judgment in any of them can lead to failure, no matter how successful a company looks on paper.

Let's explore each one in depth.

Investment Decisions: Where Money Should Be Spent

Investment decisions, also called **capital budgeting decisions**, are about **allocating resources**. They answer a simple question:

"If we have money, what is the best way to spend it to grow the business or improve operations?"

Imagine you are running a lemonade stand. You have $500 to spend. You could:

- Buy more lemons and sugar to make more lemonade
- Invest in a new juicer that increases efficiency
- Rent a second stand in a busier location

Each choice involves risk, potential reward, and opportunity cost. Corporate finance works the same way, just on a larger scale.

Examples of Investment Decisions in Real Companies

- **Opening a new store** – A retail chain must decide whether expected sales will outweigh setup costs.

- **Buying new machinery** – A factory may invest in automated equipment to reduce labor costs and improve quality.
- **Developing a new product** – Companies like Apple or Tesla invest heavily in research and development with the hope of creating something profitable.

Key Considerations

1. **Expected returns** – Will the investment earn more than it costs?
2. **Risk** – What could go wrong, and what is the chance of failure?
3. **Timing** – How long before the investment generates cash?
4. **Strategic alignment** – Does the investment fit the company's long-term goals?

Investment decisions are the **foundation of growth.** Bad investment decisions can drain a company's resources even if revenue is strong. Smart ones can multiply profits and build lasting competitive advantage.

Financing Decisions: Where Money Comes From

Once a company decides **what to invest in**, it must decide **how to pay for it**. This is where **financing decisions** come in.

A company can fund its investments from two main sources:

1. **Debt**:Borrowing money from banks, issuing bonds, or other loans.
2. **Equity**:Raising money by selling ownership shares or using retained profits.

Debt vs Equity

- **Debt** is like taking a loan to buy a car. You must repay it with interest, regardless of whether your business succeeds.
- **Equity** is like inviting a partner to buy part of your business. They share the risks and rewards.

Choosing the right mix is called **capital structure**, and it is a crucial skill for financial managers.

Real-World Example

Imagine a company wants to open a new factory costing $10 million. It can:

- Borrow the full amount from a bank (100% debt)
- Use $5 million of retained earnings and borrow $5 million (balanced approach)
- Invite investors to contribute $10 million in exchange for equity (no debt, but shares are diluted)

Each choice has consequences: debt adds repayment pressure; equity reduces ownership; using retained earnings may limit other projects.

Financing decisions are important because they affect **risk, flexibility, and long-term sustainability**. A company with too much debt may face bankruptcy during a downturn, even if its sales are strong. A company with no debt might grow more slowly but retain financial stability.

Payout Decisions: What Happens to Profits

After a company earns profits, it must decide what to do with them. This is called a **payout decision**, and it involves choices like:

- **Reinvest profits** – Use them for expansion, new projects, or paying down debt.
- **Pay dividends** – Distribute cash to shareholders as a reward for investment.
- **Buy back shares** – Reduce the number of shares in circulation to increase the value of remaining shares.

Why Payout Decisions Matter

- Reinvesting profits can fuel growth and build competitive advantage.
- Paying dividends satisfies investors and signals confidence in the company's stability.
- Buying back shares can improve metrics like earnings per share but may also signal that the company lacks growth opportunities.

Example:

- Amazon reinvested profits for years, building infrastructure, technology, and market dominance. Shareholders waited patiently, and the value of their shares skyrocketed over time.

- Coca-Cola, on the other hand, distributes steady dividends, giving investors regular income. Both strategies are valid, they simply reflect different priorities and company contexts.

Payout decisions communicate **strategy and confidence** to investors and can influence a company's valuation in the market.

How These Decisions Shape Business Survival

All three financial decisions, investment, financing, and payout are connected. A mistake in one can affect the others, and all three affect the survival and growth of a business.

Example: The High-Growth Trap

Imagine a startup that wants to expand aggressively:

1. **Investment decision:** Open 50 stores in a year.
2. **Financing decision:** Borrow heavily to fund expansion.
3. **Payout decision:** Keep all profits for reinvestment.

At first, revenue skyrockets, and the business looks successful. But the company struggles to service debt, manage costs, and keep cash flowing. Expansion stops, some stores close, and investors lose confidence.

The company fails not because the product was bad, but because the **financial decisions were misaligned and overambitious**.

Example: The Conservative Approach

A different startup grows slowly:

1. Invests only in high-return stores.
2. Uses a mix of retained profits and small loans.
3. Reinvests profits carefully.

Growth is slower, but cash flow remains healthy, debts are manageable, and investors are happy. This company survives and eventually dominates the market.

Key Insight

- **Investment decisions** determine where money is spent and potential growth.
- **Financing decisions** determine risk and sustainability.

- **Payout decisions** determine how profits are used and communicate strategy.

Companies that align all three decisions well tend to survive and thrive. Companies that neglect one often struggle, even if revenue is strong.

Key Takeaways

- Every company faces three core financial decisions: investment, financing, and payout.
- **Investment decisions** focus on where to allocate money for growth and profit.
- **Financing decisions** determine how the money is sourced and affect risk and flexibility.
- **Payout decisions** decide how profits are used or distributed.
- Poor coordination of these three decisions can lead to failure, even for companies with strong sales.
- Smart alignment of these decisions drives sustainable growth, healthy cash flow, and long-term value.

PART II

FINANCIAL STATEMENTS AS THE LANGUAGE OF BUSINESS

CHAPTER 4

Understanding Financial Statements Without Fear

If there is one thing that intimidates beginners the most in corporate finance, it is the financial statements. The income statement, balance sheet, and cash flow statement can look like a foreign language at first glance. Many professionals glance at them, nod politely, and hope someone else interprets the numbers.

The truth is that financial statements are not meant to confuse you. They exist to **tell a story about a business**. Once you understand what story they are telling, reading them becomes far less intimidating and far more powerful.

This chapter will help you understand why financial statements exist, how to interpret them, and how to avoid common beginner mistakes. By the end, you will read them like a story, not a spreadsheet.

Why Financial Statements Exist

Financial statements are the language of business. They exist to communicate financial information to decision-makers, including managers, investors, creditors, and employees.

Companies do not create statements just to satisfy accountants or regulators. They are tools to answer critical questions:

- How profitable is the business?
- How much does the company own and owe?
- Where does cash come from and where does it go?
- Can the company survive, grow, and meet its obligations?

Example:

Imagine a small bakery. The owner wants to know whether a new oven purchase will pay off. The income statement shows how much profit is being made. The balance sheet shows what the bakery owns and owes. The cash flow statement shows if there is enough cash to buy the oven and still pay staff.

Without financial statements, these answers are guesses. With them, they are informed decisions.

Key point: Financial statements are not just numbers. They are stories about money, resources, and decisions.

Performance vs Financial Position

Performance and **financial position** are two different things that are easy to confuse.

- **Performance** tells you how well the company did over a period of time, usually a month, quarter, or year. This is primarily measured in the **income statement.** Profit, revenue, and expenses show the company's results.
- **Financial position** tells you what the company owns and owes at a specific point in time. This is captured in the **balance sheet.** Assets, liabilities, and equity show the company's current standing.

Example:

A company might report $1 million in revenue this year. That sounds impressive. But if it owes $900,000 in liabilities and only has $50,000 in cash, the financial position tells a different story. Performance looks good. Position reveals risk.

Important: Focusing on just one without the other is a mistake. A profitable company can be in trouble if its financial position is weak. A company with strong assets may not survive if performance is poor.

The Role of Judgment and Estimates

Financial statements are not perfect. They are based on **judgment and estimates**, especially for items that cannot be measured precisely.

Examples of estimates in statements:

- Depreciation of equipment: Accountants estimate how long a machine will last and how much value it loses each year.
- Bad debt provisions: Companies estimate how much of their accounts receivable might not be collected.
- Inventory valuation: Companies estimate the cost of unsold goods at the end of a period.

Why this matters:

Financial statements are useful guides, not absolute truth. Understanding the assumptions behind the numbers helps you **interpret the story more accurately**. Two companies with similar revenue and profit might have very different risk profiles because of different assumptions and estimates.

How to Read Statements Like a Story

The best way to read financial statements is to think of them as a **narrative about a business**, not just numbers in a table.

Step 1: Identify the characters

- Revenue, costs, profit, assets, liabilities, cash are all characters in the story.
- Each represents an important element of the business journey.

Step 2: Understand the plot

- The income statement shows the company's journey through a period: revenue comes in, costs go out, and profit emerges.
- The balance sheet shows where the company stands at the end of that journey: what it owns and what it owes.

- The cash flow statement shows the movement of money: how much is coming in and going out to support operations, investments, and financing.

Step 3: Ask questions while reading

- Is profit growing over time?
- Are assets being used efficiently?
- Is cash flow positive and sustainable?
- Are liabilities manageable?

Step 4: Look for connections

- How does a big increase in revenue affect cash flow?
- How does investment in new equipment change assets and depreciation?
- How do financing choices affect liabilities and interest costs?

Example:

A technology company launches a new software product. The income statement shows a profit for the quarter. The balance sheet shows a large cash balance. The cash flow statement shows that most of the profit came from customer payments, not borrowed money. Reading these together, you understand that the product is truly generating value, not just paper profits.

Common Beginner Misunderstandings

1. Profit is the same as cash
Many beginners assume that a profitable company always has cash to spend. That is not true. Cash may be tied up in inventory, unpaid invoices, or loan repayments.

2. Big revenue equals a healthy business
High sales do not automatically mean financial health. Costs, debt, and cash flow matter more.

3. Financial statements are absolute truth
Remember the role of judgment and estimates. Numbers are based on assumptions, so context is key.

4. Each statement works in isolation
The income statement, balance sheet, and cash flow statement are connected. Understanding the relationships between them is essential.

5. Complex numbers are always important
Beginners often get lost in huge numbers or ratios. Focus on the story they tell, not the size of the numbers.

Key Takeaways

- Financial statements exist to tell the story of a business, not just to satisfy accountants.
- **Performance** shows results over time; **financial position** shows the current state.
- Statements rely on judgment and estimates, so understanding assumptions is critical.
- Read statements like a story: identify the characters, follow the plot, and ask questions.
- Avoid common misunderstandings: profit is not cash, revenue is not health, and numbers are context-dependent.
- Learning to read statements correctly is the foundation for all other corporate finance decisions.

CHAPTER 5

The Income Statement Made Simple

If there is one financial statement that beginners obsess over, it is the **income statement.** People often call it the profit and loss statement, or P&L, and many shy away from it because it seems full of confusing numbers and jargon.

The good news is that it does not have to be scary. The income statement is simply a **story of how a company earns money and what it costs to do business over a period of time.** Think of it as a diary for the company, showing the journey from revenue to profit.

In this chapter, we will break it down step by step. By the end, you will not just understand the income statement; you will **see it as a tool to make real business decisions.**

Revenue and Expense Recognition

Revenue is the money a company earns from its core business activities. It is often called sales, turnover, or top line.

Expense recognition is when the costs of running the business are recorded. This includes everything from raw materials to staff salaries.

Key idea: A company reports revenue **when it is earned**, not necessarily when cash is received. Similarly, expenses are recorded **when they are incurred**, not always when they are paid.

Example

Imagine a freelance graphic designer who completes a project in December for $1,000 but does not receive payment until January. According to accounting rules, the revenue is recognized in December because that is when the work was completed.

This can confuse beginners because **cash flow and revenue are not always the same thing**. Companies can appear profitable on paper even if they do not have cash in the bank yet.

Why it matters: Understanding when revenue and expenses are recognized helps you interpret whether profits are real or just timing effects.

Cost of Goods Sold and Gross Profit

Cost of Goods Sold (COGS) represents the direct costs of producing the goods or services a company sells.

- For a retailer, this is the price paid to suppliers.
- For a manufacturer, this includes materials and direct labor.
- For a service company, it might include subcontractor payments or service delivery costs.

Gross profit is calculated as revenue minus COGS. It shows how much money the company makes **before considering other operating expenses**.

Example

A bakery sells bread for $5 per loaf. The flour, yeast, and labor for each loaf cost $2.50.

- Revenue per loaf: $5
- COGS per loaf: $2.50
- Gross profit per loaf: $2.50

Gross profit is important because it shows whether the company can cover its other costs and still make a profit. If gross profit is too low, even the smartest operating decisions may not save the business.

Key point: A high revenue number is meaningless if COGS is equally high. Many beginners mistakenly equate revenue with profit.

Operating Expenses and Operating Profit

After calculating gross profit, the next step is accounting for **operating expenses**. These are costs necessary to run the business that are **not directly tied to producing goods or services**. Examples include:

- Rent and utilities
- Salaries for administrative staff
- Marketing and advertising
- Office supplies

Operating profit, also called EBIT (Earnings Before Interest and Taxes), is gross profit minus operating expenses. It measures how efficiently the company is running its core operations.

Example

Continuing with the bakery:

- Gross profit: $2.50 per loaf
- Monthly operating expenses (rent, salaries, marketing, etc.): $1,500
- Operating profit: Depends on the number of loaves sold.

If the bakery sells 1,000 loaves:

- Total gross profit: $2,500
- Operating expenses: $1,500
- Operating profit: $1,000

Operating profit is the real measure of whether the business is making money **from its main activities**, ignoring financing and taxes for now.

Key insight: Many companies can have healthy revenue but still operate at a loss if operating expenses are too high.

Net Profit and Why It Can Be Misleading

After operating profit, companies account for **non-operating items** like:

- Interest payments on loans
- Taxes owed
- Gains or losses from selling assets

What remains is **net profit**, sometimes called the bottom line.

Why net profit can be misleading

Net profit is often the number that gets most attention. Investors, journalists, and managers love to focus on it. But net profit can be **misleading for beginners**:

1. **Non-cash items** – Depreciation or amortization reduce net profit but do not involve actual cash outflow.
2. **One-time gains or losses** – Selling an old building at a gain inflates net profit for the period but is not recurring.
3. **Timing differences** – Taxes or interest payments may create spikes or dips in net profit that do not reflect ongoing operations.

Example

A tech startup reports $1 million in net profit. But closer inspection shows that $800,000 came from selling old office furniture. The company's real operating profit from its core business might only be $200,000.

Key lesson: Always look beyond net profit to understand the **true performance of the business.**

A Simple Income Statement Walkthrough

Let's put everything together using a simple example: a small online store that sells handmade candles.

Step 1: Revenue

- Candles sold: 1,000
- Price per candle: $20
- Total revenue: $20,000

Step 2: Cost of Goods Sold (COGS)

- Materials per candle: $5
- Direct labor per candle: $3
- Total COGS: $8,000
- Gross profit: $12,000

Step 3: Operating Expenses

- Rent and utilities: $2,000
- Salaries: $3,000

- Marketing: $1,000
- Total operating expenses: $6,000
- Operating profit: $6,000

Step 4: Non-Operating Items

- Interest on loan: $500
- Taxes: $1,000
- Total deductions: $1,500

Step 5: Net Profit

- Operating profit: $6,000
- Non-operating deductions: $1,500
- Net profit: $4,500

This example shows the **flow from revenue to net profit**, highlighting the impact of each step. Beginners often focus on revenue but ignoring COGS, operating expenses, and non-operating items can lead to a very misleading picture.

Tips for Reading Income Statements

- Always start at the top (revenue) and work down to net profit.
- Focus on **gross and operating profit** to understand real performance.

- Compare periods to see trends. One month's net profit does not tell the whole story.
- Look for anomalies like unusually high one-time gains or expenses.

Real-World Analogy:

Think of the income statement like a **funnel**. Revenue enters the top. Costs and expenses flow out along the way. What comes out at the bottom is the profit that remains for the owners or investors. Just because a lot of water enters the top does not mean a lot reaches the bottom. Understanding where it leaks out is crucial.

Key Takeaways

- The income statement is a story of revenue, costs, and profit over a period of time.
- Revenue is what a company earns; expenses are what it spends. Profit is the difference.
- Gross profit shows performance from production or core services. Operating profit shows performance after running the business.
- Net profit includes financing, taxes, and one-time items and can be misleading if viewed in isolation.

- Beginners should focus on trends, gross and operating profit, and the flow of money from revenue to profit.
- Always read income statements like a funnel to understand where money is earned and where it is lost.

CHAPTER 6

The Balance Sheet Explained Clearly

Every business has things it owns, things it owes, and what is left for the owners. The balance sheet is simply the snapshot that shows these three elements at a particular point in time. It is one of the most powerful tools for understanding the health and stability of a company.

While income statements show how well a business is performing over time, the balance sheet tells the story of **what the company actually has and owes right now**. Think of it like taking a photo of your financial life on a single day.

Assets: What the Company Owns

Assets are everything a company owns that has value and can help generate future profits. Assets come in two main types: **current assets** and **non-current (long-term) assets**.

Current assets are things that can be converted into cash within a year. Examples include:

- **Cash and cash equivalents** – The actual money in the bank.
- **Accounts receivable** – Money owed by customers for sales already made.
- **Inventory** – Products waiting to be sold.

Non-current assets are long-term investments and resources that support the business over multiple years. Examples include:

- **Property, plant, and equipment (PPE)** – Factories, machinery, or office buildings.
- **Intangible assets** – Patents, trademarks, or brand value.

Real-world example

Imagine a bakery:

- The cash in the register and bank account is $5,000.
- Ingredients and finished bread ready to sell (inventory) are worth $3,000.
- The bakery owns an oven and mixers worth $10,000.

Total assets: $18,000.

Assets are important because they show **what resources the company has to generate revenue.** A business with high-quality assets is better positioned to survive downturns or invest in growth.

Liabilities: What the Company Owes

Liabilities are obligations a company must settle in the future. Just like a household owes rent, loans, and utility bills, companies owe money to suppliers, lenders, employees, and tax authorities.

Liabilities are typically classified as **current** and **long-term**:

- **Current liabilities** – Obligations due within one year, such as accounts payable, wages, or taxes owed.
- **Long-term liabilities** – Debts or obligations due after more than one year, such as bank loans, bonds, or lease obligations.

Example

Back to the bakery:

- A $2,000 loan for new ovens (long-term liability).
- $1,000 owed to suppliers for flour and ingredients (current liability).

Total liabilities: $3,000.

Liabilities are not inherently bad. Borrowing money can fund growth, buy equipment, or manage cash flow. Problems arise when obligations exceed a company's ability to pay. A balance sheet helps spot these risks immediately.

Equity: Ownership and Retained Earnings

Equity represents the owners' stake in the business. It is the difference between **what the company owns (assets) and what it owes (liabilities)**. Equity can include:

- **Paid-in capital** – Money invested by owners or shareholders.
- **Retained earnings** – Profits the company keeps rather than distributing to owners as dividends.

Example

The bakery has total assets of $18,000 and total liabilities of $3,000. The equity is:

18,000 – 3,000 = $15,000

This $15,000 represents the owners' stake in the business. Part of it may have been contributed initially, and part may be accumulated profits that were reinvested.

Equity is critical because it shows **how much of the company truly belongs to the owners** and how much is financed by outside parties. Investors and creditors often look at equity to judge financial strength and risk.

Why the Balance Sheet Always Balances

The balance sheet follows the fundamental accounting equation:

Assets = Liabilities + Equity

This is why it is called a balance sheet. Everything a company owns must be financed either by borrowing (liabilities) or by owner contributions and retained profits (equity).

Example

Using the bakery:

- Assets: $18,000
- Liabilities: $3,000
- Equity: $15,000

18,000 = 3,000 + 15,000

Every asset must have a source. Even cash in the bank either came from a loan, investor funding, or profits from past operations.

Why it matters: Understanding this equation helps beginners see the relationship between what a company owns and how it is financed. It also helps explain why two seemingly identical companies might have very different financial risk profiles.

Reading Financial Strength from the Balance Sheet

The balance sheet can reveal a lot about a company's financial strength if read properly.

1. Liquidity – Can the company meet short-term obligations?

Liquidity is measured by comparing current assets to current liabilities. A simple ratio:

Current Ratio = Current Assets ÷ Current Liabilities

- Example: Bakery's current assets: $8,000 (cash, receivables, inventory)
- Current liabilities: $1,000
- Current ratio: 8,000 ÷ 1,000 = 8

This means the bakery has eight times more current assets than short-term obligations. A very strong liquidity position.

2. Solvency – Can the company meet long-term obligations?

Solvency looks at the relationship between total liabilities and equity. A company heavily financed by debt may be at higher risk in a downturn.

Debt to Equity Ratio = Total Liabilities ÷ Equity

- Bakery: $3,000 ÷ $15,000 = 0.2

A low debt-to-equity ratio shows conservative financing; a high ratio signals higher risk.

3. Asset composition – What resources support operations?

Understanding how much of the company's assets are tangible (cash, equipment) versus intangible (patents, goodwill) can indicate stability and risk. Tangible assets are easier to liquidate if needed.

4. Equity growth – Retained earnings signal reinvestment

A growing equity balance shows that profits are being retained and reinvested for growth rather than being paid out entirely as dividends.

5. Financial red flags

- Liabilities growing faster than assets or equity
- Extremely low liquidity ratios
- Heavy reliance on intangible assets with little cash

Real-world scenario

A startup technology company has assets of $1,000,000, but liabilities of $900,000, leaving only $100,000 in equity. On the surface, the company seems large, but it is heavily leveraged. A single unexpected expense could push it into insolvency.

A mature company like Johnson & Johnson has billions in assets with manageable debt and steady retained earnings. It is financially strong, resilient, and capable of surviving market fluctuations.

Visual analogy

Think of assets as the house, liabilities as the mortgage, and equity as the portion you actually own. A small house with a tiny mortgage (high equity) feels secure. A large house with a massive mortgage (low equity) can feel risky, even if the value is higher.

Key Takeaways

- The balance sheet is a snapshot of **what a company owns, owes, and the owners' stake** at a point in time.
- **Assets** are resources used to generate revenue.
- **Liabilities** are obligations owed to others, both short-term and long-term.
- **Equity** represents ownership and retained profits.
- The accounting equation ensures the balance sheet always balances: **Assets = Liabilities + Equity**.
- Liquidity, solvency, asset composition, and equity growth reveal financial strength.

- Reading the balance sheet like a story allows you to assess stability, risk, and potential for growth.

The balance sheet, when combined with the income statement and cash flow statement, gives a complete picture of a company's financial health. Understanding it lays the groundwork for more advanced topics like financial ratios, risk analysis, and valuation.

CHAPTER 7

The Cash Flow Statement and the Power of Cash

Many beginners assume that if a company is profitable, it is automatically healthy. That assumption is one of the biggest mistakes in business. Profit and cash are not the same thing. A company can appear profitable on paper while running out of money to pay its bills. Understanding the cash flow statement is essential for seeing the real financial health of a business.

The cash flow statement shows **how cash enters and leaves a company** over a period of time. While the income statement shows profit, the cash flow statement answers practical questions:

- Can the company pay employees and suppliers on time?
- Can it invest in new projects or equipment?
- Does it rely on borrowing to fund operations?

Mastering cash flow allows you to spot potential problems before they become crises and make smarter investment or operational decisions.

Why Profit Is Not the Same as Cash

Profit is an accounting concept. Cash is the actual money in the bank. While related, they can differ dramatically due to timing, non-cash items, and accounting rules.

Non-cash items like depreciation reduce profit but do not involve an actual cash outflow. A company may report $100,000 in profit, but if $50,000 of that is depreciation, the actual cash generated is less.

Timing differences also create discrepancies. Revenue is recorded when earned, but cash may arrive later. Expenses may be recorded when incurred, but payments may be delayed.

Example

A software company signs a $50,000 contract in December but receives payment in January. The income statement will show $50,000 revenue in December, but the bank account remains unchanged until January. Conversely, the company may pay a supplier $20,000 in December for next year's services, reducing cash but not profit.

Why it matters: Cash is what allows a company to survive day-to-day. Profit without cash is like having a winning lottery ticket that you cannot cash yet.

Operating Cash Flow Explained

Operating cash flow shows how much cash a company generates from its core operations. It answers the question: **Does the business generate enough cash from its normal activities to sustain itself?**

Operating cash flow starts with net profit and adjusts for **non-cash items** and **changes in working capital**. Working capital includes items like accounts receivable, inventory, and accounts payable.

Key concepts:

- **Accounts receivable** – Cash that has not yet been collected from customers reduces operating cash.
- **Inventory changes** – Buying more stock uses cash even though it does not immediately affect profit.

- **Accounts payable** – Delaying payments to suppliers can temporarily increase cash but may strain relationships.

Example

A retail store reports $100,000 net profit for the month. However:

- Accounts receivable increased by $20,000 (customers have not paid yet)
- Inventory increased by $10,000 (purchasing more goods)
- Accounts payable increased by $5,000 (suppliers not yet paid)

Operating cash flow = 100,000 – 20,000 – 10,000 + 5,000 = $75,000

Although the profit was $100,000, the actual cash generated is only $75,000. Understanding this difference is crucial for planning payments, investments, and expansion.

Practical insight: Businesses can survive lean periods with strong operating cash flow even if profits are modest. Conversely, a profitable business with poor cash flow may struggle to meet obligations.

Investing Cash Flow Explained

Investing cash flow tracks cash used for long-term investments or generated from selling assets. It reflects decisions about **growth, expansion, or divestment.**

Common items in investing cash flow include:

- **Purchasing equipment or property** – Cash outflow to support future operations.
- **Selling assets** – Cash inflow from selling equipment, property, or investments.
- **Buying or selling investments** – Cash moving in or out for stocks, bonds, or subsidiaries.

Example

A manufacturing company buys a new machine for $50,000 and sells old equipment for $10,000. Investing cash flow = 10,000 – 50,000 = -$40,000

A negative investing cash flow is not necessarily bad. It can indicate the company is investing in future growth. A positive cash flow from investing might indicate asset sales or downsizing.

Practical insight: Consistent negative investing cash flow often signals expansion and growth. Large positive flows could indicate asset liquidation or downsizing. Understanding trends helps anticipate the company's strategy.

Financing Cash Flow Explained

Financing cash flow reflects how a company raises money or returns it to investors. It answers questions about the **financial strategy and sustainability** of the business.

Common financing activities include:

- **Borrowing money** – Loans or bonds increase cash.
- **Repaying debt** – Cash outflow to settle loans or interest.
- **Issuing shares** – Raises cash by selling ownership stakes.
- **Paying dividends** – Returns cash to shareholders.

Example

A startup borrows $100,000 from a bank, repays $20,000 on a previous loan, and pays $5,000 in dividends. Financing cash flow = 100,000 – 20,000 – 5,000 = $75,000

Why it matters: Financing cash flow reveals the company's approach to growth, risk, and investor returns. Relying heavily on debt may be risky, while returning excessive dividends might limit growth potential.

Practical insight: Investors often analyze financing cash flow to assess whether a company is sustainable, aggressive, or under financial stress.

How Cash Shortages Kill Profitable Companies

Even profitable companies can fail if cash runs out. History is full of examples: companies with strong sales and reported profits going bankrupt due to poor cash management.

Real-world example 1:

A growing tech startup books $5 million in revenue and $1 million in profit. However, the company invested heavily in new equipment and expanded inventory without enough cash reserves. Suppliers demanded payment, payroll came due, and the bank loan could not cover the gap. Despite profitability, the company faced insolvency.

Real-world example 2:

Retail chains sometimes appear profitable because of high sales, but if customers delay payments or returns increase, cash flow suffers. Employees, landlords, and suppliers still need to be paid. Without enough cash, operations grind to a halt, leading to layoffs or closure.

Key lessons:

- Always monitor operating cash flow. Profit alone is not enough.
- Plan for timing gaps between cash inflows and outflows.
- Maintain cash reserves for emergencies and growth opportunities.
- Understand that investing and financing decisions affect cash availability.

Analogy: Think of a company as a boat. Profit is the size of the boat, but cash flow is the water beneath it. A large boat with no water will run aground. Managing cash ensures the boat can sail smoothly even in rough conditions.

Common cash flow pitfalls:

- Expanding too fast without sufficient cash
- Ignoring accounts receivable collections

- Relying excessively on short-term debt
- Failing to forecast cash needs accurately
- Paying out excessive dividends while investing heavily

Practical strategies to avoid cash crises:

- Forecast cash flow weekly or monthly
- Maintain a cash reserve for unexpected expenses
- Prioritize collecting receivables
- Plan investment and financing activities carefully
- Align business growth with cash availability

Key Takeaways

- Profit and cash are not the same. Cash is the lifeblood of a business.
- Operating cash flow shows the ability to generate cash from core activities.
- Investing cash flow tracks cash spent or received from long-term growth decisions.
- Financing cash flow reflects how the company raises and returns money to investors.
- Cash shortages can destroy even profitable companies. Managing cash effectively is critical for survival.

- A healthy business balances operations, investments, and financing while maintaining strong cash reserves.
- Reading cash flow alongside income and balance sheets gives a complete picture of financial health.

Real-world insight: Companies with strong cash management survive downturns, capitalize on growth opportunities, and avoid crises, even when facing challenging markets. Understanding cash flow empowers you to see beyond profits and make real decisions.

CHAPTER 8

How the Three Statements Work Together

Financial statements do not exist in isolation. The **income statement, balance sheet, and cash flow statement** are three pieces of a puzzle that together reveal the full picture of a company's health. Understanding how they interact allows you to make sense of numbers, spot risks, and evaluate business performance accurately.

How Profit Flows Into the Balance Sheet

Net profit from the income statement increases equity on the balance sheet. Retained earnings represent accumulated profits that have not been distributed to owners.

Example:

A small retail store reports $10,000 net profit for the month.

- Income statement: Revenue – Expenses = $10,000 profit
- Balance sheet: Equity increases by $10,000 through retained earnings

Without this connection, the balance sheet would not reflect the results of operations. Every dollar of profit earned eventually affects the company's financial position.

Key point: Profit on paper impacts ownership value and resources available for growth.

Cash Flow Reflects True Liquidity

Even if profit increases equity, it does not guarantee cash availability. The **cash flow statement adjusts net profit for non-cash items and changes in working capital.**

Example:

- Net profit: $10,000
- Depreciation: $2,000 (non-cash expense)
- Increase in inventory: $3,000 (cash used)
- Operating cash flow: 10,000 + 2,000 – 3,000 = $9,000

The cash flow statement ensures you know **how much money is actually available** to pay bills, reinvest, or distribute to owners.

Investing and Financing Impact Both Balance Sheet and Cash

Investing activities change the asset side of the balance sheet. Buying equipment increases assets, while selling investments converts them to cash.

Financing activities affect both **liabilities and equity**. Borrowing increases liabilities and cash. Paying dividends reduces equity and cash.

Example:

- Borrow $50,000 from the bank: Cash +$50,000, Liabilities +$50,000
- Buy machinery for $30,000: Cash –$30,000, Assets +$30,000

These activities demonstrate how cash flow movements reflect changes in both resources and obligations.

Linking the Statements for Decision Making

Step 1: Start with the income statement

- Identify profit trends and operational efficiency

Step 2: Check the balance sheet

- Assess assets, liabilities, and equity position
- Evaluate financial stability

Step 3: Review cash flow

- Ensure cash generated supports operations, investing, and financing needs
- Identify potential liquidity issues

Example:

A manufacturing company reports:

- Net profit: $100,000
- Balance sheet: $200,000 in assets, $150,000 liabilities, $50,000 equity
- Cash flow: $80,000 from operations

Even with a $100,000 profit, cash flow shows only $80,000 available. Decisions like paying suppliers, investing in equipment, or repaying debt must consider cash, not just profit.

Real-World Example of Integration

Case: A startup selling electronics online

- Month 1: Revenue $50,000, Expenses $30,000 → Net Profit $20,000
- Balance sheet: Assets $100,000 (inventory, cash), Liabilities $60,000 → Equity $40,000
- Cash flow: Operating cash flow $15,000, Investing cash flow –$10,000 (equipment), Financing cash flow $5,000 (loan)

Analysis:

- Income statement shows profit: $20,000
- Cash flow statement shows cash available for immediate use: $10,000 (15,000 – 10,000 + 5,000)
- Balance sheet reflects resources and obligations accurately: assets and equity updated

This example shows **why looking at only one statement is risky**. Decisions must be based on how all three statements interact.

Key Connections to Remember

- **Net profit → Retained earnings**: Income statement feeds equity on the balance sheet
- **Depreciation and amortization**: Reduce profit but not cash; adjusted in cash flow
- **Working capital changes**: Affect cash but not profit immediately
- **Investments and financing**: Change both cash and balance sheet items

Shortcut for beginners: Think of it as a **flow**: profit generates equity → changes affect cash → cash flows are reflected in assets and liabilities.

Key Takeaways

- Financial statements are interconnected; analyzing them together gives a complete picture.
- Profit affects equity, but cash is needed for real-world survival.
- Cash flow explains liquidity beyond profit.
- Investing and financing decisions impact both cash and balance sheet structure.
- Always review all three statements before making business decisions.
- Beginners should visualize statements as **a single system where every number influences another**.

Analogy: The income statement is the engine, the balance sheet is the chassis, and the cash flow statement is the fuel. A car may have a strong engine (profit), but without fuel (cash) or a solid chassis (balance sheet), it cannot move forward safely.

CHAPTER 9

Understanding Costs and Cost Behavior

Fixed Costs vs Variable Costs

Fixed costs are expenses that remain the same regardless of production or sales volume. Examples include: rent, salaries, insurance, and equipment leases.

Variable costs change in direct proportion to production or sales. Examples include raw materials, packaging, direct labor per unit, and sales commissions.

Example: A bakery pays $2,000 rent per month (fixed) and $1 per loaf for flour (variable).

- Producing 1,000 loaves: Total costs = Fixed $2,000 + Variable $1,000 = $3,000
- Producing 2,000 loaves: Total costs = $2,000 + $2,000 = $4,000

Key point: Understanding the mix of fixed and variable costs helps a business plan for profitability and manage financial risk.

Contribution Margin Explained Simply

Contribution margin is the difference between sales revenue and variable costs. It shows how much money is available to cover fixed costs and generate profit.

Formula: Contribution Margin = Sales Revenue – Variable Costs

Example:

- Bakery sells 1,000 loaves at \$5 each: Revenue = \$5,000
- Variable cost per loaf = \$1 → Total variable cost = \$1,000
- Contribution margin = \$5,000 – \$1,000 = \$4,000

This \$4,000 contributes to covering fixed costs (\$2,000 rent) and leaves \$2,000 profit.

Key insight: High contribution margin means each sale significantly helps cover fixed costs and improves profitability.

Cost Structure and Business Risk

A company's **cost structure** refers to the proportion of fixed and variable costs in total expenses.

- **High fixed cost structure:** Higher risk if sales drop, but higher potential profit with increased sales.
- **High variable cost structure:** Lower risk during slow periods, but profits grow more slowly when sales increase.

Example:

- Tech company: $500,000 fixed expenses (salaries, office) and low variable costs. Sales increase → profit grows rapidly. Sales drop → losses occur quickly.
- Catering business: Low fixed costs, high variable costs. Sales drop → smaller losses, but profit growth is slower when business booms.

Break-even analysis without complex math:

Break-even is the point where total revenue equals total costs (profit = $0).

Simple example:

- Fixed costs = $2,000
- Contribution margin per unit = $4
- Break-even units = Fixed Costs ÷ Contribution Margin = 2,000 ÷ 4 = 500 units

Selling 500 loaves covers all costs. Selling more = profit; selling less = loss.

Operating leverage and risk:

Operating leverage measures how sensitive profit is to changes in sales.

- High fixed costs → high operating leverage → small sales changes → large profit swings
- Low fixed costs → low operating leverage → smaller profit swings

Example:

- Bakery with high fixed costs: Rent $5,000/month
- Selling 1,000 loaves → small profit
- Selling 2,000 loaves → profit doubles or triples

Key insight: Understanding cost behavior and contribution margin helps manage pricing, plan production, and assess risk.

Key Takeaways

- Fixed costs remain constant; variable costs change with sales.
- Contribution margin shows how much revenue is available to cover fixed costs and generate profit.
- Cost structure determines financial risk and profit sensitivity.
- Break-even analysis helps identify the minimum sales needed to cover all costs.
- Operating leverage indicates how profit responds to changes in sales.
- Effective cost management improves decision-making and business stability.

PART III

COSTS, PROFITABILITY, AND BUSINESS SURVIVAL

CHAPTER 10

Measuring Performance with Financial Ratios

Financial ratios turn numbers into meaningful insights. Raw figures like revenue, profit, or debt alone rarely tell the full story. Ratios allow comparison over time, across industries, and between companies, providing a **quick snapshot of performance, efficiency, and financial health.**

Why Ratios Matter More Than Raw Numbers

Numbers by themselves can be misleading. A company may report $1 million in profit, but without context, this figure does not reveal whether the company is financially strong, efficient, or risky. Ratios standardize data and make comparisons meaningful.

Example:

- Company A: Profit = $1,000,000, Assets = $10,000,000 → Return on Assets (ROA) = 10%
- Company B: Profit = $500,000, Assets = $2,000,000 → ROA = 25%

Raw numbers suggest Company A is bigger, but Company B is more efficient at using its assets to generate profit.

Ratios provide clarity in areas such as:

- Profitability – How well a company generates income
- Liquidity – Can the company meet short-term obligations?
- Debt management – How much risk does the company carry?
- Operational efficiency – How effectively resources are used

Understanding ratios helps stakeholders, investors, and managers **spot strengths, weaknesses, and potential problems early**.

Profitability Ratios That Actually Matter

Profitability ratios measure the company's ability to generate earnings relative to revenue, assets, or equity.

1. Gross Profit Margin

Shows how efficiently a company produces goods or services.

Formula: Gross Profit ÷ Revenue × 100

Example:

- Revenue = $100,000
- Cost of Goods Sold (COGS) = $60,000
- Gross Profit = $40,000
- Gross Profit Margin = 40%

A higher margin indicates better efficiency and pricing strategy.

2. Operating Profit Margin

Measures profit after operating expenses but before interest and taxes.

Formula: Operating Profit ÷ Revenue × 100

Example:

- Revenue = $100,000
- Operating expenses = $20,000
- Operating Profit = $20,000
- Operating Profit Margin = 20%

3. Net Profit Margin

Shows the final profit after all expenses, including taxes and interest.

Formula: Net Profit ÷ Revenue × 100

Example:

- Net Profit = $15,000
- Revenue = $100,000
- Net Profit Margin = 15%

4. Return on Assets (ROA)

Indicates how efficiently a company uses assets to generate profit.

Formula: Net Profit ÷ Total Assets × 100

Example:

- Net Profit = $50,000
- Total Assets = $500,000
- ROA = 10%

5. Return on Equity (ROE)

Measures profitability relative to shareholders' equity.

Formula: Net Profit ÷ Equity × 100

Example:

- Net Profit = $50,000

- Equity = $200,000
- ROE = 25%

Key insight: Investors use ROA and ROE to gauge efficiency and returns. Higher percentages indicate better performance but may also imply higher risk depending on debt levels.

Liquidity and Debt Ratios Explained

Liquidity ratios measure the ability to cover short-term obligations. Debt ratios measure how much of the company's financing comes from debt versus equity.

1. Current Ratio

Measures if current assets cover current liabilities.

Formula: Current Assets ÷ Current Liabilities

Example:

- Current Assets = $50,000
- Current Liabilities = $25,000
- Current Ratio = 2

A ratio above 1 indicates the company can meet short-term obligations. Too high may suggest idle cash or inefficient asset use.

2. Quick Ratio

Similar to current ratio but excludes inventory, focusing on the most liquid assets.

Formula: (Current Assets – Inventory) ÷ Current Liabilities

Example:

- Current Assets = $50,000
- Inventory = $20,000
- Current Liabilities = $25,000
- Quick Ratio = (50,000 – 20,000) ÷ 25,000 = 1.2

A ratio above 1 is generally safe.

3. Debt-to-Equity Ratio

Shows how much debt a company uses relative to equity.

Formula: Total Liabilities ÷ Equity

Example:

- Liabilities = $100,000
- Equity = $200,000
- Debt-to-Equity = 0.5

Lower ratios indicate conservative financing; higher ratios indicate higher risk.

4. Interest Coverage Ratio

Measures the company's ability to pay interest on debt from operating profit.

Formula: Operating Profit ÷ Interest Expense

Example:

- Operating Profit = $50,000
- Interest Expense = $10,000
- Interest Coverage = 5

A ratio below 1.5–2 may signal financial stress.

Using Ratios to Spot Danger Early

Ratios help detect problems before they become crises.

Signs of trouble:

- Declining gross profit margin → rising production costs or falling prices
- Low current ratio → liquidity problems
- High debt-to-equity ratio → overleveraging
- Declining ROA → inefficient asset use

Example:

A retail chain has:

- Current ratio: 0.8 → may struggle to pay suppliers
- Debt-to-equity: 3 → highly leveraged, risky in downturns
- Net profit margin: falling from 15% to 8% → shrinking profitability

By monitoring ratios, management can act early: reduce debt, cut costs, or improve operations.

Trend analysis: Comparing ratios over multiple periods provides better insight than a single number.

Industry comparison: Ratios are more meaningful when compared to industry benchmarks.

Practical tip: Focus on the ratios that matter most for your business type:

- Retail: Gross margin, inventory turnover, current ratio
- Manufacturing: Operating margin, ROA, debt-to-equity
- Service: Net margin, ROE, operating leverage

Key Takeaways

- Ratios transform raw numbers into actionable insights.
- Profitability ratios reveal efficiency at generating profit.
- Liquidity ratios measure short-term financial health.
- Debt ratios assess financial risk and leverage.
- Tracking trends and comparing to benchmarks helps spot danger early.
- Using ratios consistently allows better decision-making, forecasting, and strategy.
- No single ratio tells the whole story; the combination of profitability, liquidity, and debt ratios gives a full picture.

CHAPTER 11

Profitability, Growth, and Sustainable Performance

Profitability vs Growth

Profitability measures how effectively a company converts revenue into profit. **Growth** measures how quickly a company increases revenue, assets, or market share. Both are important, but they do not always move together.

Example:

A tech startup earns $50,000 profit on $200,000 revenue (profit margin 25%). It decides to expand aggressively, doubling sales to $400,000 but spending heavily on marketing and hiring. Profit drops to $10,000. Revenue growth increased, but profitability suffered.

Key point: High growth without attention to profit can strain cash, increase costs, and reduce long-term value.

Why Fast Growth Can Destroy Value

Rapid expansion can be risky:

- **Cash strain:** Higher sales often require more inventory, staffing, and working capital.
- **Operational stress:** Systems, processes, and management may not keep up.
- **Quality decline:** Rushed production or service delivery can hurt reputation.
- **Debt accumulation:** Companies may borrow heavily to fund growth, increasing financial risk.

Example:

A restaurant chain opens five new locations in one year. Revenue doubles, but cash outflows for rent, equipment, and staff leave the business short of funds. Suppliers demand payment, and one location closes due to poor operations. Growth happened, but value was destroyed.

Key insight: Growth must be balanced with operational capacity, cash flow, and profitability.

Sustainable Growth in Plain Language

Sustainable growth is the pace at which a company can grow without taking on excessive risk or sacrificing profitability.

Principles of sustainable growth:

- **Profit-driven expansion:** Use retained earnings and operational cash rather than excessive debt.
- **Controlled scaling:** Open new locations or enter new markets gradually.
- **Maintain efficiency:** Ensure systems, processes, and staffing can handle growth.
- **Monitor metrics:** Track profitability, cash flow, and debt levels continuously.

Example:

A boutique clothing brand increases sales by 15% per year while keeping profit margins steady. New store openings are carefully planned based on cash flow, staffing, and demand. Growth is steady, risk is controlled, and value increases over time.

Key point: Sustainable growth protects the business from overextension while building long-term profitability and value.

Key Takeaways

- Profitability and growth are different: both are needed, but one can affect the other.
- Rapid growth without careful planning can destroy value.
- Sustainable growth balances expansion, profitability, and operational capacity.
- Focus on using internal resources and cash flow for growth whenever possible.
- Monitoring key financial metrics ensures growth supports long-term business health.

PART IV

FINANCIAL RATIOS: MAKING NUMBERS USEFUL

CHAPTER 12

Why Financial Ratios Matter

Limits of Absolute Numbers

Absolute numbers like revenue, net profit, or total debt show the size of a business but **tell little about efficiency, risk, or financial health**. Two companies with the same revenue can be worlds apart in profitability, liquidity, and sustainability.

Example:

- Company A: Revenue $1,000,000, Net Profit $50,000 → Net Profit Margin = 5%
- Company B: Revenue $500,000, Net Profit $50,000 → Net Profit Margin = 10%

Both companies made $50,000 profit, but Company B is twice as efficient at generating profit from sales. Absolute numbers hide this crucial insight.

Why it matters:

- Investors may overestimate larger companies based on size alone.
- Management may miss operational inefficiencies.
- Creditors may not see underlying liquidity problems.

Key insight: Ratios provide **context and clarity** that raw numbers cannot. They allow you to compare efficiency, performance, and risk in a meaningful way.

Comparing Companies Using Ratios

Ratios allow apples-to-apples comparison across companies of different sizes or industries. They standardize financial information to reveal relative performance.

Profitability ratios:

- **Gross Margin**: Measures production efficiency. Higher margins indicate better cost control.
- **Net Margin**: Shows overall profitability after all expenses.
- **ROA**: Shows how effectively assets generate profit.

- **ROE**: Measures return for shareholders.

Liquidity ratios:

- **Current Ratio**: Ability to meet short-term obligations.
- **Quick Ratio**: Focuses on most liquid assets, excluding inventory.

Debt ratios:

- **Debt-to-Equity Ratio**: How much leverage a company uses.
- **Interest Coverage Ratio**: Ability to service debt from operating profits.

Example:

- Company A: Revenue $2,000,000, Net Profit $200,000 → Net Margin = 10%, Debt-to-Equity = 1.5
- Company B: Revenue $1,500,000, Net Profit $150,000 → Net Margin = 10%, Debt-to-Equity = 0.5

Although net margins are identical, Company B is less leveraged and financially safer. Without ratios, you might assume Company A is stronger simply because it is larger.

Benchmarking: Ratios also allow comparison with **industry averages**, helping to see if a company is above or below peers.

Example:

A retail chain has a gross margin of 30% while the industry average is 25%. The company is performing efficiently. If net margin lags behind the industry, it may indicate high operating costs or mismanagement.

Using Ratios to Spot Red Flags

Financial ratios act as early warning signals. Trends over time or unusual deviations from industry norms often highlight **potential problems before they become crises.**

Profitability red flags:

- Declining gross or net margin → rising costs, pricing pressure, or inefficiencies
- ROA or ROE decreasing → assets or equity not generating enough profit

Liquidity red flags:

- Current ratio below 1 → may struggle to pay short-term obligations
- Quick ratio below 0.8 → reliance on inventory or delayed collections

Debt-related red flags:

- Debt-to-equity rising rapidly → increasing financial risk
- Interest coverage below 2 → difficulty meeting interest payments

Example:

A manufacturing firm reports:

- Current ratio falling from 1.5 to 0.9 over six months
- Net margin declining from 12% to 6%
- Debt-to-equity rising from 1 to 2.5

Interpretation: The company may face liquidity issues, profitability is declining, and leverage is increasing. Immediate action may be required to reduce debt, improve cash flow, or control costs.

Trend analysis:

Ratios are most powerful when analyzed over time. Short-term fluctuations may occur due to seasonality or one-time events, but consistent patterns indicate deeper operational or financial issues.

Example:

- A retail chain shows increasing gross margin for three years but decreasing net margin.
- Interpretation: Production efficiency improved, but operating expenses or overhead are growing too quickly. Action: Cost review, efficiency measures, or restructuring.

Practical tip for beginners:

- Focus on **a small set of key ratios** relevant to your business.
- Track ratios monthly or quarterly to detect trends early.
- Compare ratios against **industry standards** for context.
- Use ratios to guide **decisions about investment, cost management, and financing.**

Key Takeaways

- Absolute numbers alone cannot reveal efficiency, risk, or sustainability.
- Ratios allow meaningful comparisons across companies of different sizes.
- Profitability ratios show how well a company converts revenue into profit.
- Liquidity ratios highlight the ability to meet short-term obligations.
- Debt ratios reveal financial leverage and risk.
- Trend analysis and benchmarking are essential for spotting early warning signs.
- Ratios are powerful tools to make informed, data-driven business and investment decisions.

CHAPTER 13

Profitability Ratios Explained Clearly

Gross Margin

Gross margin measures how efficiently a company produces or delivers its goods and services. It shows the percentage of revenue left after covering the **cost of goods sold (COGS)**.

Formula:
Gross Margin = (Revenue – COGS) ÷ Revenue × 100

Example:

- Revenue = $200,000
- COGS = $120,000
- Gross Margin = (200,000 – 120,000) ÷ 200,000 × 100 = 40%

Key point: A higher gross margin indicates better efficiency and pricing power. It reflects how much money is available to cover operating expenses and generate profit.

Practical insight: Retailers often aim for high gross margins to protect against fluctuations in sales volume or supplier costs. Service companies may have lower gross margins but offset with lower fixed costs.

Operating Margin

Operating margin measures the percentage of revenue left after covering **operating expenses**, such as salaries, rent, marketing, and utilities. It reflects core business profitability before interest and taxes.

Formula:
Operating Margin = Operating Profit ÷ Revenue × 100

Example:

- Revenue = $200,000
- Operating Expenses = $50,000
- Operating Profit = 200,000 – 120,000 (COGS) – 50,000 = $30,000
- Operating Margin = 30,000 ÷ 200,000 × 100 = 15%

Key point: Operating margin shows how well a company controls costs while running its core operations.

Practical insight: Businesses with strong operating margins can withstand price pressure, economic downturns, or cost increases better than low-margin competitors.

Net Profit Margin

Net profit margin measures the percentage of revenue that remains as profit **after all expenses**, including interest and taxes. It represents the ultimate efficiency of the business in converting revenue into actual profit.

Formula:
Net Profit Margin = Net Profit ÷ Revenue × 100

Example:

- Revenue = $200,000
- Total Expenses (COGS + Operating + Taxes + Interest) = $170,000
- Net Profit = 30,000
- Net Profit Margin = 30,000 ÷ 200,000 × 100 = 15%

Key point: Net profit margin is a key indicator for investors and owners because it shows the true profitability of the company.

Practical insight: A rising net margin over time signals improved efficiency or pricing, while a falling margin may indicate rising costs, declining revenue, or inefficient operations.

Interpreting Profitability Trends

Tracking profitability ratios over time reveals **business performance trends**. It is not enough to look at a single period.

Example:

- Year 1: Gross Margin 40%, Operating Margin 15%, Net Margin 10%
- Year 2: Gross Margin 38%, Operating Margin 12%, Net Margin 8%
- Year 3: Gross Margin 36%, Operating Margin 10%, Net Margin 5%

Interpretation: Costs are increasing faster than revenue growth. The business is becoming less efficient and may need cost control, pricing review, or operational improvements.

Trend analysis tips:

- Compare ratios year over year to identify improvement or decline.
- Benchmark against industry standards to assess relative performance.
- Combine with other ratios like ROA and ROE to understand the impact on overall financial health.

Key insight: Consistent improvement in profitability ratios indicates a healthy, efficient business. Declining ratios signal a need for corrective action before problems become serious.

Key Takeaways

- **Gross margin** shows efficiency in producing goods or delivering services.
- **Operating margin** highlights core operational profitability before interest and taxes.
- **Net profit margin** reveals final profit efficiency after all expenses.
- Profitability trends over time help identify improvements, risks, and areas needing action.
- Comparing ratios to industry benchmarks provides context and ensures realistic assessments.

- Monitoring all three profitability ratios together gives a complete picture of performance.

CHAPTER 14

Liquidity and Solvency Ratios

Current Ratio

Current ratio measures a company's ability to meet its short-term obligations using its current assets.

Formula:
Current Ratio = Current Assets ÷ Current Liabilities

Example:

- Current Assets = $60,000
- Current Liabilities = $30,000
- Current Ratio = 60,000 ÷ 30,000 = 2

Key point: A ratio above 1 indicates that the company has more current assets than liabilities and can cover short-term debts.

Practical insight: A very high ratio may suggest that the company is not using its assets efficiently. A very low ratio signals liquidity risk.

Quick Ratio

Quick ratio, also called the acid-test ratio, measures liquidity without relying on inventory, which may take time to convert into cash.

Formula:
Quick Ratio = (Current Assets – Inventory) ÷ Current Liabilities

Example:

- Current Assets = $60,000
- Inventory = $20,000
- Current Liabilities = $30,000
- Quick Ratio = (60,000 – 20,000) ÷ 30,000 = 1.33

Key point: A quick ratio above 1 generally indicates the company can pay off immediate obligations without relying on selling inventory.

Practical insight: Businesses with high inventory turnover can rely on current ratio, but cash-sensitive companies benefit more from monitoring the quick ratio.

Debt-to-Equity Ratio

Debt-to-equity ratio measures financial leverage and shows the proportion of debt and equity financing the company uses.

Formula:
Debt-to-Equity = Total Liabilities ÷ Shareholders' Equity

Example:

- Total Liabilities = $80,000
- Equity = $120,000
- Debt-to-Equity = 80,000 ÷ 120,000 = 0.67

Key point: Lower ratios indicate conservative financing, while higher ratios suggest higher financial risk.

Practical insight: Investors and lenders watch this ratio closely. Too much debt may be dangerous during economic downturns.

Short-Term vs Long-Term Financial Risk

Short-term financial risk is the risk of not meeting current obligations (liquidity risk).

- Indicators: Low current ratio, low quick ratio, late payments, overdrafts
- Impact: Operational disruptions, supplier issues, damaged reputation

Long-term financial risk relates to the company's ability to sustain operations with its debt structure (solvency risk).

- Indicators: High debt-to-equity, low interest coverage, declining equity
- Impact: Higher borrowing costs, restricted growth, risk of bankruptcy

Example:

- A retail chain: Current ratio 0.9 → short-term liquidity concern
- Debt-to-equity 3 → high long-term leverage
- Action: Reduce debt, improve cash reserves, monitor liabilities

Key insight: Liquidity ratios protect against day-to-day crises, while solvency ratios ensure the company can survive over the long term. Both must be analyzed together for a complete picture of financial health.

Key Takeaways

- **Current ratio** shows ability to meet short-term obligations.
- **Quick ratio** provides a stricter measure of liquidity, excluding inventory.
- **Debt-to-equity ratio** reveals leverage and long-term risk.
- Short-term risk (liquidity) and long-term risk (solvency) require different strategies.
- Monitoring these ratios helps prevent financial crises and supports sustainable growth.
- Both liquidity and solvency must be considered before making investment or lending decisions.

CHAPTER 15

Efficiency Ratios and Asset Utilization

Asset Turnover

Asset turnover measures how efficiently a company uses its assets to generate revenue. Higher ratios indicate better use of resources.

Formula:
Asset Turnover = Revenue ÷ Total Assets

Example:

- Revenue = $500,000
- Total Assets = $250,000
- Asset Turnover = 500,000 ÷ 250,000 = 2

Key point: Every dollar invested in assets generates $2 in revenue. A higher ratio suggests the company is efficient in using its assets to generate sales.

Practical insight: Companies with high asset turnover can generate strong revenue without heavy investment in assets, creating a competitive advantage.

Inventory Turnover

Inventory turnover measures how quickly a company sells and replaces inventory over a period. It reflects efficiency in managing stock.

Formula:
Inventory Turnover = Cost of Goods Sold ÷ Average Inventory

Example:

- COGS = $120,000
- Average Inventory = $30,000
- Inventory Turnover = 120,000 ÷ 30,000 = 4

Interpretation: The company sells and replaces its inventory four times per year.

Key point: High turnover indicates efficient inventory management, reducing holding costs and risk of obsolescence. Low turnover may signal slow-moving stock or poor demand planning.

Practical insight: Retailers and manufacturers rely heavily on inventory turnover to optimize cash flow and operational efficiency.

Efficiency and Competitive Advantage

Efficiency ratios reveal **how well a company uses resources** compared to competitors.

Example:

- Company A: Asset turnover = 2.5, Inventory turnover = 6
- Company B: Asset turnover = 1.5, Inventory turnover = 3

Company A is more efficient, generating more revenue from each dollar of assets and selling inventory faster. This efficiency may allow lower pricing, higher profitability, or faster reinvestment.

Key insight: High efficiency creates a competitive advantage by reducing costs, improving responsiveness, and maximizing returns from assets.

Tips for improving efficiency:

- Streamline operations to reduce idle assets

- Optimize inventory levels using demand forecasting
- Invest in technology and processes that increase productivity
- Regularly benchmark against competitors or industry averages

Key Takeaways

- **Asset turnover** shows how effectively assets generate revenue.
- **Inventory turnover** measures how efficiently stock is sold and replaced.
- High efficiency improves cash flow, profitability, and competitiveness.
- Benchmarking efficiency ratios against peers helps identify strengths and weaknesses.
- Consistently monitoring efficiency ratios supports better operational decisions and sustainable growth.

PART V

TIME, RISK, INVESTMENT DECISIONS

CHAPTER 16

The Time Value of Money Made Intuitive

Why Money Today Is Worth More Than Money Tomorrow

Imagine someone promises to give you $100 today or $100 one year from now. Which would you choose? Almost everyone picks **today**, and the reason is simple: **money now is more valuable than money later**. This principle is at the heart of corporate finance and is called the **time value of money (TVM).**

Why is this true? There are three main reasons: opportunity cost, inflation, and risk.

Opportunity Cost: Money in hand today can be invested, earning a return. Waiting a year means losing the chance to grow your money.

Inflation: Prices rise over time, so $100 today buys more goods and services than $100 a year from now.

Risk: There is uncertainty about the future. A promise to pay later may never be fulfilled, making future money less reliable.

Analogy: Think of money like seeds. A seed planted today grows into a tree. Waiting a year to plant the seed delays the harvest and reduces total growth.

In business, this principle is critical. Companies use it to evaluate investments, decide when to borrow, and understand the real value of future cash flows. Ignoring the time value of money can lead to poor financial decisions, overvalued projects, or missed opportunities.

Opportunity Cost Explained

Opportunity cost is the value of the best alternative you give up when choosing one option over another. In finance, it is the return you could have earned on your money if invested elsewhere.

Example:

- You have $1,000. Option A: Spend it on a new phone. Option B: Invest in a savings account at 5% annual interest.

- Choosing Option A costs you $50 in potential interest over one year. That $50 is the opportunity cost.

In corporate finance, opportunity cost is **central to investment decisions**.

Example:

- Company X has $500,000. It can invest in Project A expected to earn $60,000 or Project B expected to earn $50,000. Choosing Project B over A incurs an opportunity cost of $10,000.

Opportunity cost also applies to **time and resources**, not just money. Spending resources on one project means they are unavailable for another, potentially more profitable venture.

Practical insight: Every financial decision has a cost in terms of lost opportunities. Evaluating alternatives using opportunity cost ensures resources are allocated to maximize value.

Inflation and Purchasing Power

Inflation is the rise in prices over time, which erodes the purchasing power of money. A dollar today buys more than a dollar tomorrow.

Example:

- Coffee today costs $2.
- With 5% annual inflation, the same coffee will cost $2.10 next year.

Implication: Receiving $100 in the future is not equivalent to having $100 today. You need to **adjust future money to today's value** to make accurate financial decisions.

Real-world scenario:

- A company expects to receive $100,000 from a contract in 5 years. If inflation averages 3% per year, the purchasing power of that $100,000 will only be equivalent to about $86,000 today.

Ignoring inflation can make investments seem more profitable than they truly are. Companies must consider inflation when evaluating long-term projects, pricing strategies, and financial forecasts.

Key point: Inflation reminds us that the **nominal value of money** is different from its **real value**, which reflects actual purchasing power.

Risk and Uncertainty Over Time

Money promised in the future carries **risk**. There is always uncertainty about whether it will be received, how economic conditions will change, or whether the investment will perform as expected.

Example:

- Lending $1,000 to a friend with a 50% chance of repayment is riskier than lending to a bank. Future money is not guaranteed, so it is less valuable than money in hand.

In corporate finance, companies discount future cash flows to account for risk. Higher uncertainty → higher discount rate → lower present value.

Practical insight: Even highly profitable projects are evaluated considering risk. A project promising $1 million in five years is not automatically worth $1 million today. Its value depends on how certain and safe that cash is.

Analogy: Think of future money like walking across a narrow bridge over a river. The farther away you are, the riskier the journey. Money today is already on solid ground; future money may fall into uncertainty.

Compounding and Discounting Without Pain

Compounding is how money grows over time when it earns interest. The longer it remains invested, the more it grows, not just on the original amount, but on accumulated interest as well.

Example:

- Invest $1,000 at 10% annual interest:
  - Year 1: $1,000 × 10% = $100 → Total = $1,100
  - Year 2: $1,100 × 10% = $110 → Total = $1,210

Key insight: Compounding accelerates growth. The earlier you invest, the more time your money has to grow.

Discounting is the reverse: determining what a future amount is worth today.

Example:

- You will receive $1,100 in 1 year. If the interest rate is 10%, the present value (today's worth) = $1,100 ÷ (1 + 0.10) = $1,000

Why it matters: Present value lets companies compare projects, investments, or cash flows occurring at different times. It turns the future into a value we can evaluate today.

Real-world application:

- A company is considering two projects:
  - Project A: Earn $50,000 next year
  - Project B: Earn $60,000 in two years
- Using a discount rate of 10%:
  - Project A PV = 50,000 ÷ 1.10 = $45,455
  - Project B PV = 60,000 ÷ (1.10^2) = 60,000 ÷ 1.21 = $49,587

Project B seems higher in nominal terms, but when adjusted for the time value of money, Project B is only slightly better. Decisions depend on **both timing and risk-adjusted value.**

Opportunity Cost, Inflation, and Risk Combined

Time value of money combines these three forces:

1. **Opportunity cost** ensures money could have earned elsewhere.
2. **Inflation** reduces purchasing power over time.
3. **Risk** accounts for uncertainty in receiving the money.

Example:

- A company has $100,000 and can invest in:
    - Government bonds (low risk, low return)
    - Stock market (higher risk, higher return)
- Inflation averages 3% annually.
- Expected returns: Bonds 5%, Stocks 10%

Calculating present value allows comparing these options on an apples-to-apples basis, accounting for growth, risk, and inflation.

Practical insight: Smart managers always evaluate future cash flows, considering these three factors. Ignoring any one can lead to poor investment choices, overpaying for acquisitions, or undervaluing future opportunities.

Real-World Applications of Time Value of Money

Investment decisions:

- Companies use TVM to calculate Net Present Value (NPV) and Internal Rate of Return (IRR) when deciding which projects to pursue.

Loan and debt management:

- Banks and borrowers use TVM to calculate monthly payments, interest, and total cost of loans.

Pricing and contracts:

- Long-term contracts, lease agreements, or deferred payments are discounted to their present value for fair pricing.

Personal finance:

- Retirement planning, savings, and investment growth all rely on understanding compounding and discounting.

Example:

A startup evaluates two investment offers:

- Investor A offers $100,000 today for 10% equity
- Investor B offers $120,000 in two years for 15% equity

Using a discount rate of 10% to calculate present value, management can decide which offer is financially better today.

Making Time Value of Money Intuitive

Rule of thumb: Money now is worth more than the same amount later.

- Invest early → compounding multiplies growth
- Consider risk → adjust expectations for uncertainty
- Account for inflation → ensure real purchasing power is maintained

Analogy: Think of money as water in a reservoir. Today's water is in your tank; tomorrow's may leak through pipes or evaporate. Using and growing it now is safer and more productive.

Simple mindset:

- Future cash = today's cash × growth factor (adjusted for risk and inflation)
- Present value = future cash ÷ (1 + discount rate)^number of periods

Even without complex formulas, the principle is simple: **early, safe, and productive money is far more valuable than delayed, uncertain money**.

Key Takeaways

- Money today is always worth more than money tomorrow due to opportunity cost, inflation, and risk.
- Opportunity cost represents the returns foregone by not investing money elsewhere.
- Inflation erodes purchasing power over time.
- Risk and uncertainty reduce the value of future money.
- Compounding allows money to grow faster over time; discounting converts future amounts to present value.
- Time value of money underpins investment decisions, loan management, project evaluation, and strategic planning.
- Understanding TVM equips individuals and businesses to make smarter, more profitable

decisions, balancing growth, risk, and timing effectively.

CHAPTER 17

Present Value and Future Value Without Complexity

Compounding Explained Intuitively

Compounding is the process of **growing money over time by earning interest on both the original amount and previously earned interest.** It is what makes investments powerful and savings multiply.

Example:

- You invest \$1,000 at 10% interest per year.
    - Year 1: \$1,000 × 10% = \$100 → Total = \$1,100
    - Year 2: \$1,100 × 10% = \$110 → Total = \$1,210
    - Year 3: \$1,210 × 10% = \$121 → Total = \$1,331

Notice how the interest earned each year grows because it accumulates on top of prior interest. This is often called **"interest on interest."**

Analogy: Think of compounding like rolling a snowball down a hill. It starts small, but as it rolls, it picks up more snow and grows faster the bigger it gets.

Practical insight: Compounding rewards **early action and patience**. The sooner you start investing or saving, the more your money grows over time.

Discounting Explained Intuitively

Discounting is the reverse of compounding. It is the process of **determining the present value of money to be received in the future**. It answers the question: how much is a future cash flow worth today?

Example:

- You will receive \$1,210 in 2 years. If the interest rate is 10%, the present value (today's equivalent) = $\$1,210 \div (1 + 0.10)^2 = \$1,210 \div 1.21 \approx \$1,000$

Key point: Discounting allows you to **compare cash flows at different points in time** on the same scale, today's value.

Analogy: Think of future money like a promise of water delivered tomorrow. Due to uncertainty and inflation, that water is worth less today than if it were in your tank right now. Discounting helps calculate its true value in today's terms.

Practical insight: Businesses use discounting to **evaluate projects, investments, and contracts.** Receiving $100,000 five years from now is not equivalent to having $100,000 today; discounting accounts for time, risk, and opportunity cost.

Practical Business Applications

1. Investment Decisions:

- Companies calculate **Net Present Value (NPV)** to decide whether a project adds value.
- Only projects where the present value of cash inflows exceeds outflows are considered worthwhile.

Example:

- Project requires $50,000 today and will generate $60,000 in 2 years.
- Discount rate = 10%
- Present value of $60,000 = $60{,}000 \div (1 + 0.10)^2 \approx$ $49,587
- NPV = 49,587 – 50,000 = –$413 → Project slightly negative, may be rejected.

2. Loan Management:

- Calculating **monthly payments** or **total interest** relies on understanding PV and FV.
- Banks discount future loan payments to determine how much money they are effectively earning today.

3. Pricing and Deferred Payments:

- Businesses offering **credit or delayed payments** adjust prices using discounting to account for the time value of money.
- This ensures the company is compensated for giving money later instead of now.

4. Retirement and Long-Term Planning:

- Individuals use PV and FV to plan savings, ensuring money grows enough to meet future goals.
- Compounding shows the benefit of starting early; discounting shows how much you need to invest today for a future target.

Example:

- Target: $100,000 in 10 years
- Interest rate: 8% per year
- Present value = $100{,}000 \div (1 + 0.08)^{10} \approx \$46{,}319$
- You need to invest $46,319 today to reach $100,000 in 10 years.

Key insight: PV and FV are **tools for decision-making**, helping businesses and individuals compare today's money with future amounts, account for risk, and make financially sound choices.

Key Takeaways

- **Compounding** grows money over time by earning interest on interest.
- **Discounting** determines today's value of future money, accounting for time, risk, and opportunity cost.
- Early action and understanding PV/FV can multiply returns and prevent costly mistakes.
- Businesses use PV and FV for investment evaluation, loan management, pricing, and long-term planning.
- Mastering these concepts allows you to see **the real value of cash flows over time** and make smarter financial decisions.

CHAPTER 18

Making Smart Investment Decisions

What Counts as a Business Investment

A business investment is any use of money or resources intended to generate a future benefit or return. It is **not just buying equipment or opening a new branch**, it includes anything that adds value to the company over time.

Examples:

- Purchasing machinery that improves production
- Investing in employee training to increase productivity
- Launching a new marketing campaign to attract customers
- Developing software or technology for long-term efficiency

Key insight: An investment is about **using resources today to earn more in the future**, not just spending money.

Practical tip: Always ask: *Will this action generate more value than it costs?* If yes, it's a potential investment. If no, it may be a cost disguised as investment.

Risk vs Return Trade-Offs

Every investment carries **risk**, which is the chance that actual returns will differ from expected returns. Understanding the trade-off between risk and reward is crucial.

Low-risk investments typically offer steady, smaller returns:

- Example: Government bonds, savings accounts
- Predictable, low uncertainty, but low growth

High-risk investments offer higher potential returns but greater uncertainty:

- Example: Startups, stock market, experimental projects
- Returns can be large, but failure is possible

Illustration:

- A company invests $100,000 in a secure bond earning 5% → guaranteed $5,000 a year

- Same $100,000 in a startup could return $50,000, nothing, or even lose part of the investment

Key point: Smart investment decisions balance **potential reward with acceptable risk**, based on the company's strategy and capacity to absorb losses.

Capital Budgeting Logic (Payback, NPV, IRR , Conceptually)

Capital budgeting is the method companies use to evaluate and prioritize investment projects.

1. Payback Period:

- Measures how long it takes to recover the initial investment
- Shorter payback = quicker return of money
- Limitation: Ignores cash flows beyond the recovery period and time value of money

Example: Invest $50,000 in equipment expected to generate $10,000 per year → Payback = 50,000 ÷ 10,000 = 5 years

2. Net Present Value (NPV):

- Calculates the **present value of expected future cash flows minus the investment cost**
- Positive NPV = project expected to add value
- Negative NPV = project destroys value

Example: Invest \$50,000 to earn \$60,000 in 2 years. Discount future cash flows at 10% → Present value = 60,000 ÷ 1.21 ≈ 49,587 → NPV ≈ –413 → Slightly negative, may reject

3. Internal Rate of Return (IRR):

- The rate at which a project's NPV equals zero
- Higher IRR than required return → acceptable project
- Lower IRR → reject project

Key insight: These tools help companies **compare projects of different sizes and timelines**. They make investment decisions more structured and less emotional.

Why Good-Looking Projects Get Rejected

Not all projects that seem profitable are accepted. Companies reject projects for several reasons:

- **Insufficient cash flow:** Even profitable projects can strain finances
- **High risk:** Returns may be attractive but uncertainty is too great
- **Strategic misalignment:** The project doesn't fit company goals or expertise
- **Better alternatives:** Capital is limited; higher-value projects take priority
- **Time constraints:** Payback period may be too long relative to company needs

Example: A company may reject a project promising $500,000 profit over 10 years because the initial investment ties up cash needed for faster-growing opportunities.

Practical insight: Smart investing is **not about chasing the highest return**, but about maximizing **value relative to risk, timing, and strategic fit.**

Key Takeaways

- Business investments include anything that uses resources today to generate future value.

- All investments involve risk; higher potential return comes with higher uncertainty.
- Capital budgeting tools like Payback, NPV, and IRR help evaluate projects systematically.
- Projects that look profitable may be rejected if they strain cash, are too risky, or conflict with strategy.
- Making smart investment decisions requires balancing **profit, risk, timing, and strategic alignment**.
- Monitoring investments and learning from outcomes is crucial to improving decision-making over time.

CHAPTER 19

Debt, Equity, and the Cost of Capital

Where Companies Get Money

Companies need funds to grow, operate, and invest. Money comes from two primary sources: **debt** and **equity**. Understanding the characteristics, costs, and implications of each is essential for making smart financial decisions.

- **Debt:** Borrowed money that must be repaid with interest
- **Equity:** Capital raised from owners or investors in exchange for ownership stakes

Key insight: The choice between debt and equity impacts risk, control, and the company's financial flexibility.

Debt Financing Explained Simply

Debt financing means borrowing money from banks, lenders, or bond investors. It is a **contractual**

obligation, and companies must repay both principal and interest.

Advantages of Debt:

- Interest payments are tax-deductible, reducing effective cost
- Does not dilute ownership; founders retain control
- Predictable repayment schedule

Risks of Debt:

- Fixed repayment obligations create financial pressure
- High leverage increases risk of insolvency if cash flow falls
- Excessive debt can limit future borrowing capacity

Example:

- A company borrows $100,000 at 8% interest per year.
- Annual interest = $8,000, principal must eventually be repaid.
- If operations generate steady cash flow, the company benefits from leverage.

- If sales drop, debt obligations may strain finances.

Practical insight: Debt works well for companies with stable cash flow, predictable revenues, or short-term financing needs.

Equity Financing and Ownership Dilution

Equity financing means raising money by selling shares of the company to investors. In return, investors become partial owners.

Advantages of Equity:

- No fixed repayment obligations
- Brings in additional resources, expertise, or connections
- Reduces financial risk compared to debt

Trade-Offs:

- Ownership dilution: Founders give up a portion of control and profits
- Dividend expectations: Investors may expect regular returns
- Decision-making: More voices in governance

Example:

- A startup raises $200,000 by selling 20% equity to investors.
- Founders retain 80% ownership.
- The capital can fund expansion without increasing debt obligations.

Practical insight: Equity is ideal for businesses in early stages, high-risk ventures, or those requiring substantial upfront investment.

Choosing the Right Mix of Financing

The combination of debt and equity is called **capital structure**. Choosing the right mix balances **risk, cost, and control**.

Considerations:

- **Cost of capital:** Debt is cheaper because interest is tax-deductible, but too much increases financial risk.
- **Control:** Equity avoids debt obligations but dilutes ownership.
- **Flexibility:** A balanced mix ensures funding availability without overburdening the company.

Example:

- Company A uses 70% debt, 30% equity → low ownership dilution but high leverage risk
- Company B uses 30% debt, 70% equity → lower risk but more ownership shared with investors

Practical insight: Optimal financing depends on the company's industry, growth stage, cash flow stability, and strategic goals. Conservative industries (utilities, manufacturing) can support more debt, while high-growth tech startups often rely more on equity.

Key Takeaways

- Companies fund operations and growth through **debt and equity**.
- **Debt financing** provides leverage but increases financial risk due to repayment obligations.
- **Equity financing** reduces risk but dilutes ownership and control.
- The **capital structure**, the mix of debt and equity, affects cost, risk, and flexibility.
- Choosing the right financing mix requires balancing **risk tolerance, cost of capital, and strategic objectives**.

- Understanding financing options empowers companies to grow sustainably and make informed financial decisions.

PART VI

FINANCING THE BUSINESS

CHAPTER 20

Risk, Return, and Decision-Making

Business Risk vs Financial Risk

When companies make decisions, understanding the **types of risk** is critical. Risk affects not only potential returns but also survival and long-term growth. Broadly, there are two main types of risk: **business risk** and **financial risk**.

Business risk arises from the day-to-day operations of a company. It is about uncertainty in **revenues, costs, and profitability**. Every business faces it, no matter how large or established.

Sources of Business Risk:

- **Market demand fluctuations:** A sudden drop in customer demand can reduce sales.
- **Competition:** New entrants or aggressive competitors can affect market share.
- **Operational issues:** Supply chain disruptions, production failures, or labor strikes.
- **Regulatory changes:** New laws or taxes can increase costs or limit operations.

Example: A coffee shop chain faces a business risk if a new competitor opens nearby. Even if the business has a loyal customer base, some customers may switch, affecting revenue.

Financial risk arises from how a company is financed, specifically the **use of debt**. Companies that rely heavily on borrowing are exposed to financial risk because interest payments and loan repayments are mandatory.

Sources of Financial Risk:

- **High leverage:** Borrowing large amounts increases the risk of insolvency if cash flow falls.
- **Interest rate changes:** Rising rates increase repayment costs for variable-rate loans.
- **Refinancing risk:** Difficulty in securing new financing can jeopardize operations.

Example: The same coffee shop borrows $500,000 to expand. Even if sales drop slightly, it still owes fixed monthly payments. If the cash isn't enough, the company may default.

Key difference:

- Business risk is about **uncertainty in operations**, independent of financing.
- Financial risk is about **uncertainty due to how the business is financed**.

Practical insight: Companies with stable cash flows and predictable operations can take on more financial risk safely. Startups or businesses with volatile revenues should limit borrowing and focus on operational efficiency first.

Analogy: Business risk is like walking on uneven terrain, you might stumble because of the environment. Financial risk is like carrying a heavy backpack while walking, you are more likely to fall even if the terrain is flat.

Risk Premium Explained Simply

Investors expect **compensation for taking risks**. This is called the **risk premium**.

Definition: Risk premium is the extra return above a "safe" or risk-free rate that investors require for taking on additional uncertainty.

Example:

- A government bond offers 3% return (considered risk-free).
- A startup investment is expected to return 12%.
- Risk premium = 12% – 3% = 9%

Key point: The higher the uncertainty, the higher the risk premium required.

Why it matters:

- Helps companies understand **cost of capital**. Riskier businesses must offer higher returns to attract investors.
- Guides **investment decisions**. Projects with higher risk must provide higher expected returns to justify the investment.

Factors Affecting Risk Premium:

1. **Business volatility:** Companies in cyclical industries (construction, luxury goods) require higher premiums.
2. **Financial leverage:** Highly indebted companies are riskier, increasing required return.
3. **Market uncertainty:** Economic downturns or political instability raise expected risk premiums.

Example:

- Company A: Stable utility company → expected return 7% → Risk premium 4% over risk-free rate
- Company B: Tech startup → expected return 20% → Risk premium 17% over risk-free rate

Analogy: Investing in a startup is like boarding a small boat on the ocean during a storm. The extra thrill (risk) demands extra reward (premium) for the danger involved. A calm, predictable river ride (government bond) requires little extra reward.

Practical insight: Understanding risk premiums helps managers set realistic expectations, avoid overpaying for projects, and balance risk and return strategically.

Making Decisions Under Uncertainty

Uncertainty is inevitable in business. Even the best forecasts can be wrong. Making decisions under uncertainty requires **structured thinking** and awareness of risk.

Step 1: Identify Risks

- List operational, market, financial, and regulatory risks.
- Assess which risks can be mitigated and which are unavoidable.

Step 2: Quantify Risks

- Estimate potential impacts on cash flow, profits, and survival.
- Use ranges instead of single numbers to account for variability.

Step 3: Consider Expected Returns

- Compare expected benefits with potential risks.
- Incorporate **risk premiums** to adjust expected returns for uncertainty.

Step 4: Explore Alternatives

- Look for options that **reduce risk while maintaining return**.
- Diversification: spreading investments across products, markets, or projects.

- Hedging: using contracts or insurance to protect against specific risks.

Step 5: Decide and Monitor

- Make informed choices based on **risk-return trade-offs**.
- Monitor actual outcomes and adjust strategies as needed.

Example:

- A company considers expanding to a new country.
  - Business risks: unknown market, local competition, cultural differences
  - Financial risks: borrowing for expansion, currency fluctuation
  - Expected return: additional $1 million profit per year

The company may:

- Choose a phased entry to reduce risk
- Partner with a local business to share risk
- Use conservative financing to limit financial exposure

Practical tip: Decisions under uncertainty are rarely perfect. The goal is to **balance potential upside with manageable risk** and plan contingencies.

Analogy: Making business decisions under uncertainty is like hiking in fog. You cannot see the entire path, but with proper preparation, maps, and cautious steps, you can reach your destination safely.

Risk and Return in Everyday Business

Investment decisions:

- Projects with higher volatility require higher expected returns.
- Low-risk, stable projects may be preferred if cash flow is tight or financial obligations are high.

Financing decisions:

- Choosing debt vs equity involves weighing financial risk.
- High debt amplifies potential returns but also increases the chance of default.

Operational decisions:

- Diversifying products or markets reduces business risk.
- Insurance, safety measures, and quality control protect against operational failures.

Example:

- Company X has $1 million to invest. Options:
    - Invest in a steady government bond → 3% return, low risk
    - Expand to a high-growth but volatile market → 15% expected return, high risk
- Decision depends on cash reserves, appetite for risk, and long-term strategy.

Key insight: Risk is not inherently bad. It is the **price of opportunity**. Understanding risk, quantifying it, and managing it allows businesses to pursue higher returns while avoiding catastrophic outcomes.

Decision-Making Tools Under Uncertainty

1. **Scenario Analysis:** Evaluate best-case, worst-case, and most-likely outcomes.

2. **Sensitivity Analysis:** Assess how changes in one variable affect results.
3. **Expected Value Calculation:** Weight possible outcomes by probability to estimate average expected return.
4. **Risk Adjusted Discount Rate:** Increase the discount rate for higher-risk projects to reflect uncertainty.

Example:

- Project expected to earn $500,000 with 70% probability and lose $100,000 with 30% probability.
- Expected value = (0.7 × 500,000) + (0.3 × -100,000) = 350,000 – 30,000 = $320,000

Practical insight: Using these tools helps **make rational, data-driven decisions** rather than relying on gut feeling alone.

Business Risk vs Financial Risk in Real Life

Case 1: Business Risk dominates

- Retailer faces declining foot traffic due to e-commerce trends.
- Limited debt → financial risk is low.

- Action: Reduce costs, diversify sales channels, innovate products.

Case 2: Financial Risk dominates

- Manufacturing company takes on large debt for expansion.
- Stable operations, but high interest obligations.
- Action: Focus on maintaining cash flow, refinance debt if possible, avoid additional borrowing.

Case 3: Both risks high

- Startup launches in a new, competitive industry with borrowed capital.
- Action: Consider phased investment, risk-sharing partnerships, or delaying expansion until some stability is achieved.

Key lesson: Understanding the dominant type of risk informs **where to focus mitigation strategies.**

Sources of Business Financing

Understanding where companies get money is critical for making smart financial decisions. Financing is not just about raising cash, it shapes risk, control, and future growth. Companies generally use two broad sources of financing: **internal financing** and **external financing**. Both come with trade-offs that affect how the business operates and grows.

Internal Financing

Internal financing is money generated **from within the company**, usually from retained earnings, depreciation funds, or cost-saving measures. Essentially, it's using the company's own resources to fund operations or investments rather than borrowing or selling equity.

Key Sources of Internal Financing:

- **Retained Earnings:** Profits that are kept in the business instead of paid as dividends.
    - Example: A company earns $500,000 in profit but distributes $200,000 to shareholders. The remaining $300,000 can be reinvested to purchase equipment or expand operations.
- **Depreciation Funds:** Non-cash accounting expenses like depreciation create "booked" cash that can be redirected for reinvestment.

    - Example: A company records $50,000 depreciation on machinery. That money isn't actually spent but is available to replace old equipment.
- **Cost Savings and Efficiency Gains:** Money saved from reducing waste or improving processes can be reinvested.
    - Example: Streamlining production cuts $20,000 in annual expenses. This saved cash becomes an internal source for other projects.

Advantages of Internal Financing:

- **No debt obligation:** No interest payments or repayment schedules.
- **No ownership dilution:** Founders and shareholders retain full control.
- **Low risk:** Using existing cash reduces the chance of insolvency.

Limitations:

- **Limited availability:** Only as much cash as the company generates or saves can be used.
- **Slower growth:** Rapid expansion may require more funds than internally available.

- **Opportunity cost:** Using profits internally means shareholders cannot receive dividends or invest elsewhere.

Practical Insight: Internal financing is ideal for **stable, profitable businesses** that want to grow without increasing risk or giving up ownership. It encourages discipline, as projects must be funded from actual resources rather than borrowed money.

External Financing

External financing is money raised **from outside the company**, either by borrowing or selling ownership stakes. This is essential when internal funds are insufficient for growth, expansion, or unexpected expenses.

Two main types of external financing:

1. **Debt Financing:** Borrowing money that must be repaid with interest.
2. **Equity Financing:** Raising money by selling shares of the company to investors.

Debt Financing

Debt financing can come from banks, financial institutions, bonds, or even family and friends. It involves a contractual obligation to repay principal plus interest.

Advantages:

- **Retains ownership:** The company keeps full control; lenders do not get voting rights.
- **Tax benefits:** Interest payments are often tax-deductible.
- **Predictable costs:** Payments are fixed and can be planned.

Risks and Limitations:

- **Repayment obligations:** Even if the company makes no profit, debt must be repaid.
- **Financial risk:** High leverage increases the chance of insolvency.
- **Cash flow pressure:** Regular payments reduce flexibility for operations or new projects.

Example:

- A company borrows $500,000 at 8% annual interest for new machinery. Interest = $40,000/year. If sales drop, the company must still pay the $40,000, creating financial stress.

Practical Insight: Debt is suitable for companies with **stable, predictable cash flow** and established operations. Borrowing allows faster growth but must be balanced with repayment capacity.

Equity Financing

Equity financing involves selling part of the company to investors. Investors provide capital in exchange for **ownership stakes**, sharing in profits and potentially influencing decisions.

Advantages:

- **No repayment pressure:** Unlike debt, money raised does not need to be repaid.
- **Risk sharing:** Investors share the financial risk of the business.
- **Additional resources:** Investors may bring expertise, networks, or credibility.

Trade-offs:

- **Ownership dilution:** Founders give up a portion of control and profits.
- **Expectations of returns:** Investors may expect dividends or growth.
- **Decision influence:** Shareholders may demand input into major business decisions.

Example:

- A startup raises \$1 million by selling 25% equity to investors. Founders retain 75% ownership but gain capital to launch operations.

Practical Insight: Equity is best for **high-growth, high-risk businesses** or startups that cannot generate sufficient internal funds or bear significant debt.

Choosing Between Debt and Equity

The decision between debt and equity depends on:

- **Cost of capital:** Debt is cheaper due to tax deductibility, but excessive debt increases financial risk.
- **Ownership control:** Equity dilutes control but reduces repayment pressure.
- **Business stability:** Stable businesses can handle more debt; volatile businesses benefit from equity.
- **Strategic goals:** Expansion speed, growth expectations, and investor involvement influence choice.

Example:

- Company A: Stable utility firm → can safely use 60% debt, 40% equity
- Company B: Tech startup → uses 20% debt, 80% equity to reduce risk

Practical Tip: Many successful businesses use a **mix of debt and equity**, called **capital structure**, to balance risk, cost, and control.

The True Cost of Capital

Understanding the **true cost of financing** is critical. It is not just interest or dividends, it's the overall cost of using funds to generate returns.

Cost of Debt:

- Interest paid on loans minus tax benefits.
- Example: $100,000 loan at 8% interest, tax rate 30% → After-tax cost = 8% × (1 – 0.3) = 5.6%

Cost of Equity:

- Expected return demanded by shareholders.
- Example: Investors expect 12% return → Cost of equity = 12%

Weighted Average Cost of Capital (WACC):

- Companies often combine debt and equity costs to determine the overall cost of capital.
- Formula (conceptual): WACC = (Proportion of Debt × Cost of Debt) + (Proportion of Equity × Cost of Equity)
- Helps decide whether an investment will generate sufficient returns to justify financing.

Practical Insight:

- Projects should generate returns higher than the true cost of capital to create value.
- Using cheaper debt can lower overall costs, but over-reliance increases risk.
- Equity avoids repayment stress but is "more expensive" in terms of ownership dilution and expected returns.

Internal vs External Financing: Strategic Considerations

FACTOR	INTERNAL FINANCING	EXTERNAL FINANCING

Control	Full control retained	Ownership shared
Repayment	No repayment required	Debt must be repaid; equity has investor expectations
Cost	Low (opportunity cost only)	Debt: interest; Equity: expected return
Availability	Limited by internal cash	Can raise large amount externally
Risk	Low financial risk	Debt increases risk; equity shares risk

Decision-making insight: Companies should first use internal financing for smaller or low-risk projects and consider external sources for larger, high-return investments. A balanced approach optimizes growth without jeopardizing stability.

Practical Examples of Financing Decisions

1. **Expanding Production:**
- Internal: Use retained earnings to buy a second production line → low risk, slower growth.
- Debt: Borrow to buy multiple lines → faster growth, higher financial risk.
- Equity: Bring in investors → growth with less repayment pressure, but share profits.

2. **Launching a New Product:**
- Internal: Fund from savings → safe, but limited marketing budget.
- External: Use a mix of debt and equity → allows robust launch, spreads risk, but requires repayment or profit sharing.

3. **Covering Short-Term Cash Needs:**
- Internal: Delay non-critical expenses → low cost, temporary fix.
- Debt: Short-term loan → fast, but interest costs and repayment pressure.
- Equity: Rarely used for short-term needs → expensive in terms of ownership dilution.

Key Takeaways

- Companies fund operations and growth through **internal and external financing**.
- **Internal financing** uses retained earnings, depreciation, or savings → low risk, no repayment, preserves control.
- **External financing** comes from **debt** (borrowing) or **equity** (selling ownership).
- Debt is cheaper but increases financial risk; equity avoids repayment stress but dilutes ownership.
- Understanding the **true cost of capital** ensures investments generate returns above the financing cost.
- Smart financing involves a **balanced mix** to optimize growth, minimize risk, and maintain flexibility.
- Decisions about financing should consider **control, repayment obligations, cost, availability, and risk**.

Final Insight: Mastering financing sources and their costs empowers businesses to grow sustainably, seize opportunities, and weather challenges without compromising stability or ownership.

Loans and Bonds in Simple Terms

Debt financing is borrowing money to fund business activities, projects, or expansion. It comes in two main forms: **loans** and **bonds**. Both involve a promise to repay the borrowed amount (principal) with interest.

Loans:

- Money borrowed from banks, financial institutions, or private lenders.
- Usually comes with a fixed repayment schedule over months or years.
- Interest rates can be fixed or variable.
- Can be short-term (less than a year) or long-term (more than a year).

Example: A company borrows $100,000 from a bank to buy new equipment, agreeing to repay over five years at 8% annual interest.

Bonds:

- A bond is like a loan from multiple investors instead of a bank.
- The company agrees to pay a fixed interest (coupon) over the bond's life and repay the principal at maturity.
- Bonds are often traded on financial markets.

Example: A company issues $1 million in bonds with a 6% annual coupon for 10 years. Investors lend the money in exchange for interest payments, and the company repays the principal after 10 years.

Key Insight: Both loans and bonds allow companies to access capital without giving up ownership. The choice depends on the size of the financing, cost, and flexibility required.

Interest, Repayment, and Default Risk

Interest is the cost of borrowing money. It compensates the lender or investor for the risk and opportunity cost of providing funds.

Repayment schedules are critical. Companies must plan cash flow to meet regular interest and principal payments. Missing payments can lead to penalties, damaged credit ratings, or legal action.

Default Risk is the chance the company cannot meet its debt obligations. High default risk increases borrowing costs because lenders demand higher interest to compensate for the risk.

Example:

- Company A borrows $200,000 at 5% interest. The annual payment is $10,000. If cash flow drops and the company cannot pay, the lender may seize collateral or take legal action.
- Company B issues bonds with a high coupon of 12% because investors perceive the company as risky. Higher interest compensates investors but increases the company's financial burden.

Practical Insight: Proper planning ensures companies do not over-leverage and can meet obligations even during downturns.

Analogy: Borrowing is like taking a car on credit. You gain access immediately but must make regular payments. Miss too many payments, and you risk losing the car and damaging your credit.

Benefits and Dangers of Debt

Benefits:

1. **Leverage for Growth:** Debt allows companies to invest in projects that may generate higher returns than the cost of borrowing.
2. **Tax Advantage:** Interest payments are often tax-deductible, lowering the effective cost.

3. **Retain Ownership:** Unlike equity, debt does not dilute ownership or control.

Example: A company borrows $500,000 at 6% to buy equipment expected to generate $100,000 extra annual profit. If profit exceeds interest, the company benefits from leverage.

Dangers:

1. **Financial Risk:** High debt increases the chance of insolvency if cash flow falls.
2. **Fixed Obligations:** Regular payments reduce flexibility for other opportunities or emergencies.
3. **Bankruptcy Risk:** Failure to meet obligations can lead to legal consequences or loss of assets.

Real-World Example:

- Many companies have failed despite strong revenue because they over-leveraged. For instance, retailers sometimes borrow heavily to expand during boom years. If sales drop, debt obligations may force them into bankruptcy.

Practical Strategies to Use Debt Wisely:

- Match the **loan term** with the expected life of the project.
- Keep **interest coverage ratios** in check, ensure profits can comfortably cover interest.
- Maintain a **cash reserve** for unexpected downturns.
- Avoid over-leveraging; balance debt with equity for flexibility.

Key Takeaways:

- Debt financing provides capital without giving up ownership but carries repayment obligations and default risk.
- Loans are direct borrowings from institutions; bonds raise money from investors.
- Interest and repayment schedules must be managed carefully to avoid financial distress.
- Using debt wisely can accelerate growth, but over-reliance can endanger the company.

Equity Financing and Ownership

Shares and Ownership Rights

Equity financing is raising money by selling **shares** of a company. When investors buy shares, they become

part-owners of the business and have certain rights, depending on the type of shares they hold.

Types of Rights Typically Granted to Shareholders:

- **Voting rights:** Influence key decisions like electing the board of directors, approving major investments, or mergers.
- **Dividend rights:** Entitlement to a portion of company profits when dividends are declared.
- **Residual claims:** In the event of liquidation, shareholders receive assets after debts are paid.
- **Preemptive rights:** Existing shareholders may have the option to buy new shares before outsiders to maintain ownership percentage.

Example:

- A startup issues 1,000 shares. An investor buys 250 shares, owning 25% of the company. They gain proportional rights to profits, voting, and a say in major business decisions.

Practical Insight: Shares represent both **ownership and responsibility**. Investors bear the risk of losses but benefit from profits and growth in company value.

Analogy: Owning a share is like owning a slice of a pie. You have a claim on your slice's portion, and you share in decisions about how the pie is made, eaten, or divided.

Dilution Explained Clearly

Dilution occurs when a company issues new shares, reducing existing shareholders' ownership percentage. It does not always reduce the value of existing shares, but it does affect control and profit share if additional capital is not used effectively.

Example:

- Original setup: Company has 1,000 shares. You own 250 shares → 25% ownership.
- New shares issued: 500 additional shares sold to raise capital.
- Total shares now: 1,500. Your 250 shares now represent **16.7% ownership**.

Key Points About Dilution:

- **Control:** Voting power is reduced; decisions may shift in influence.

- **Profit share:** Earnings per share (EPS) may decline unless new capital creates additional profits.
- **Strategic impact:** Dilution is sometimes necessary to fund growth, hire talent, or bring in strategic partners.

Practical Insight: Wise investors and founders monitor dilution carefully, ensuring that **new capital generates value greater than the ownership lost.**

Analogy: Imagine owning a 25% slice of a cake. If the baker adds more cake for others, your slice becomes a smaller percentage unless you also get extra. If the new cake makes the overall cake bigger, your slice may still be worth more in absolute terms.

Private vs Public Equity

Equity can be raised in two main ways: **private** and **public.**

Private Equity:

- Money is raised from private investors, such as angel investors, venture capitalists, or private equity firms.
- Shares are not traded publicly.

- Often involves close collaboration, mentorship, or strategic guidance from investors.

Example: A startup raises $1 million from three angel investors in exchange for 30% equity. These investors may provide advice, connections, and guidance beyond just money.

Public Equity:

- Shares are sold to the public through stock exchanges.
- Requires strict regulatory compliance, reporting, and transparency.
- Provides access to large amounts of capital but also subjects the company to market scrutiny.

Example: A technology firm goes public, offering 10 million shares to raise $50 million. Shareholders can buy and sell freely, and the company must regularly report performance and financials.

Advantages of Public Equity:

- Access to significant capital for expansion.
- Liquidity for shareholders.
- Market visibility and credibility.

Disadvantages:

- Loss of privacy and control.
- Pressure to meet quarterly expectations.
- Regulatory compliance costs and obligations.

Advantages of Private Equity:

- Flexible terms, tailored to company needs.
- Investors may provide expertise and mentorship.
- Less public scrutiny and regulatory burden.

Disadvantages:

- Limited pool of capital.
- Exit options may be slower.
- Investors may have significant control depending on agreements.

Practical Insight: Startups often begin with private equity to grow without market pressure. Established firms may turn to public equity to scale rapidly or provide liquidity for existing investors. Choosing the right route depends on **growth strategy, control preferences, and funding needs**.

Capital Structure and Financial Flexibility

The Debt-Equity Trade-Off

Every company must decide **how much to finance with debt versus equity**. This decision defines its **capital structure** and directly impacts risk, control, and financial flexibility.

Debt Advantages:

- Lower cost of capital due to tax-deductible interest.
- Retains ownership and control.
- Can amplify returns on profitable projects (financial leverage).

Debt Disadvantages:

- Fixed obligations increase financial risk.
- Over-reliance can lead to insolvency if cash flows falter.

Equity Advantages:

- No mandatory repayments, reducing financial stress.
- Shares bring in investors who may add expertise and networks.

Equity Disadvantages:

- Dilutes ownership and control.
- Investors expect returns, which may limit cash available for reinvestment.

Example:

- Company A wants to invest $1 million in expansion.
    - Debt option: Borrow $1 million at 6% → fixed interest payments.
    - Equity option: Sell 20% of the company → no repayment, but ownership shared.
    - Decision depends on current cash flow, risk tolerance, and control priorities.

Practical Insight: The trade-off is about **balancing cost, risk, and control**. Companies aim to optimize returns while keeping financial obligations manageable.

Financial Leverage Explained

Financial leverage occurs when a company uses debt to finance projects. Proper leverage can magnify profits, but it also increases risk.

Example:

- A company invests $100,000 of its own money in a project and earns $20,000 → 20% return.
- If it borrows $100,000 at 5% interest to invest $200,000 in total:
    - Project earns $40,000.
    - Interest = $5,000.
    - Net profit = $35,000 → return on equity = 35% instead of 20%.

Benefit: Leverage increases return on equity when projects earn more than the cost of debt.

Risk: If the project earns less than the interest cost, leverage amplifies losses.

Practical Insight: Leverage should match the company's **cash flow stability**. Stable businesses can safely use higher leverage, while volatile firms benefit from low debt levels.

Analogy: Think of leverage like using a lever to lift a heavy object. It can make the lift easier and more effective, but if you misjudge the force, the lever can snap and cause bigger problems.

Why There Is No Perfect Capital Structure

Many books promise a "perfect debt-to-equity ratio," but the truth is there isn't one. Optimal capital structure depends on:

- **Industry norms:** Utilities may safely carry more debt; tech startups usually require more equity.
- **Cash flow stability:** Companies with predictable income can take on more debt.
- **Growth strategy:** Aggressive expansion may require more equity to reduce financial stress.
- **Market conditions:** Interest rates, investor sentiment, and economic cycles affect borrowing costs and capital availability.

Practical Insight:

- Capital structure is dynamic, not fixed. Companies adjust debt and equity levels over time.
- The goal is **flexibility**: having enough liquidity and borrowing capacity to pursue opportunities while avoiding excessive risk.

Example:

- A manufacturer may start with mostly equity financing in its early years. As revenues stabilize, it may add moderate debt to fund a large expansion.

- A retail chain with predictable cash flow may maintain 50% debt and 50% equity to minimize cost while staying flexible for future growth.

Key Takeaways:

- The debt-equity mix defines financial risk, cost of capital, and control.
- Financial leverage can magnify profits but increases vulnerability if projects underperform.
- There is no one-size-fits-all capital structure; flexibility and adaptability are more important than any "ideal ratio."
- Companies must continuously assess cash flow, growth plans, and market conditions to maintain a sustainable capital structure.

PART VII

VALUATION AND VALUE CREATION

CHAPTER 21

What a Company Is Really Worth

Understanding the true value of a business is central to corporate finance. Many beginners confuse **price** with **value**, relying on accounting numbers or market hype. The reality is more nuanced: a company's worth is determined by its ability to generate **cash flows, manage risks, and sustain growth over time.**

Price vs Value

Price is what someone is willing to pay for a company today. It can be influenced by market sentiment, speculation, or temporary trends.

Value, on the other hand, reflects the company's **intrinsic ability to generate cash and create wealth over the long term.**

Example:

- A tech startup receives a $10 million offer from an investor. That is the **price.**

- After analyzing expected future cash flows, growth potential, and risks, the management estimates the **intrinsic value** at $7 million.
- Paying $10 million above intrinsic value may be overpriced and risky, while paying below $7 million could represent a bargain.

Practical Insight: Price is observable, but value requires careful analysis. Focusing on value helps avoid overpaying or undervaluing opportunities.

Analogy: Price is like the ticket cost to enter a concert; value is the enjoyment and experience you gain from attending.

What Drives Business Value

Business value is primarily driven by the company's ability to **generate future cash flows**, manage risk, and maintain competitive advantage. Key drivers include:

- **Revenue growth:** Consistent increase in sales over time.
- **Profit margins:** Ability to generate cash from revenue efficiently.
- **Cash flow stability:** Predictable inflows and outflows reduce risk and increase value.

- **Competitive advantage:** Unique products, strong brand, patents, or market position protect future earnings.
- **Operational efficiency:** Lower costs or better resource utilization enhances profitability.
- **Management quality:** Experienced, capable leadership makes better decisions and mitigates risk.

Example:

- Two companies have $1 million in revenue.
    - Company A has a 5% profit margin, inconsistent cash flow, and high competition.
    - Company B has a 15% profit margin, stable cash flow, and a strong brand.
    - Despite equal revenue, Company B is more valuable because it generates more reliable profit and cash flow.

Practical Insight: Value comes from **sustainable cash generation**, not just accounting profits or sales figures.

Cash Flow Thinking vs Accounting Profit

Accounting profit is calculated according to rules like **matching revenue and expenses** or **depreciation**. While useful for reporting, it doesn't always reflect cash available to the business.

Cash flow thinking focuses on **actual money moving in and out**. Investors and managers rely on cash flow to:

- Pay employees and suppliers
- Service debt
- Fund new projects
- Distribute dividends

Example:

- A company reports $100,000 profit on its income statement.
- Accounts receivable increased by $50,000, meaning cash hasn't been collected.
- Inventory increased by $20,000, using cash to buy stock.
- Actual cash generated = $100,000 – $50,000 – $20,000 = $30,000

Even with a high accounting profit, the company has only $30,000 in usable cash.

Practical Insight: Cash flow drives **real value** because it determines whether the business can survive, invest, and grow.

Why Valuation Is Not Exact

Valuation is inherently **imperfect** because it involves estimating the future under uncertainty. Several factors make exact valuation impossible:

- **Forecasting uncertainty:** Future revenue, costs, and cash flows are estimates, not guarantees.
- **Changing market conditions:** Competition, regulations, and economic cycles can alter expected value.
- **Discount rates and assumptions:** Deciding how to value future cash flows involves assumptions about risk, inflation, and opportunity cost.
- **Intangible factors:** Brand value, employee talent, and customer loyalty are difficult to quantify precisely.

Example:

- Two analysts value the same company using discounted cash flow methods.
- Analyst A assumes 10% growth, Analyst B assumes 7%.
- Valuations differ significantly, yet both are reasonable based on their assumptions.

Practical Insight: Valuation is a **range, not a single number**. Successful investors and managers focus on reasonable ranges, underlying assumptions, and sensitivity to changes rather than exact figures.

Analogy: Valuation is like predicting the weather. You can estimate likely temperatures and conditions, but exact outcomes are uncertain. You plan based on ranges, risks, and probabilities.

Real-World Example: Cash Flow Thinking and Value

- **Company X** has \$5 million revenue and \$1 million profit, but it relies heavily on delayed customer payments and holds excess inventory. Its cash flow is unstable, reducing value.
- **Company Y** has \$3 million revenue and \$500,000 profit but collects cash immediately and keeps inventory low. Its cash flow is consistent, making it more valuable than Company X despite lower accounting profit.

Key Takeaways:

- **Price ≠ Value:** Always distinguish between what you pay and what the company is intrinsically worth.

- **Value comes from cash flows, not just profits or revenue.**
- **Strong, predictable cash flows increase valuation.**
- **Valuation involves assumptions; it is always a range, not an exact number.**
- **Competitive advantage, operational efficiency, and quality management amplify value.**

Practical Strategy for Beginners:

- Focus on **cash-generating capacity** rather than just profits.
- Use **multiple methods** to estimate value: discounted cash flow, comparable companies, and precedent transactions.
- Always test sensitivity: see how value changes if revenue, margins, or growth assumptions vary.
- Remember that value is dynamic. A company's worth changes with market conditions, management decisions, and execution of strategy.

Cash Flow-Based Valuation (Beginner Level)

Valuing a business using **cash flows** is one of the most powerful and practical ways to understand what a company is truly worth. Unlike accounting profit or revenue, cash flows show the **actual money moving in and out**, which directly determines the company's ability to survive, grow, and create wealth.

Why Cash Flows Drive Value

Cash flows are the lifeblood of any business. While profit can be influenced by accounting rules, non-cash items, or one-time events, **cash flow reflects reality**, the money the company can spend, invest, or distribute to shareholders.

Key Points:

- Investors pay for **future cash flows**, not historical profits.
- A company with strong, stable cash flows is more valuable than a company with high accounting profits but poor cash generation.
- Cash flow allows companies to:
  - Pay employees and suppliers
  - Service debt
  - Fund growth and expansion
  - Return money to shareholders

Example:

- Company A reports $1 million in profit, but most customers pay 90 days later, leaving only $200,000 in cash.
- Company B reports $500,000 in profit but collects cash immediately, leaving $500,000 available to invest or distribute.
- Despite lower accounting profit, Company B is **more valuable** because its cash flow is more reliable.

Analogy: Think of cash flow as the water flowing through a pipe, and profit as the volume of water promised by the meter. Without actual flow, the system can't function, no matter what the meter says.

Practical Insight: Cash flow-based valuation aligns value with what the business can realistically deliver in terms of liquidity and growth.

Discounted Cash Flow Intuition

Discounted Cash Flow (DCF) is a valuation method that estimates **the present value of future cash flows.** While traditional DCF calculations can seem complicated, the core idea is simple:

Money today is worth more than money tomorrow due to opportunity cost, inflation, and risk.

Step-by-step intuition:

1. **Estimate future cash flows:** Predict how much cash the business will generate each year.
    - Example: $100,000 next year, $120,000 the year after, and so on.
2. **Adjust for risk and time:** Future cash is less valuable than cash today. The further in the future, the less certain it is.
    - Example: $100,000 next year might be worth $95,000 today; $120,000 in two years might be worth $105,000 today.
3. **Sum the present values:** Adding up all adjusted cash flows gives the company's estimated value.

Simple Analogy:

- Imagine lending $100 today to a friend. You expect repayment in a year, but because money could have earned interest elsewhere, that $100 next year is worth less to you than $100 today. DCF applies the same principle to businesses.

Practical Example:

- A small business expects cash flows:
    - Year 1: $50,000
    - Year 2: $60,000
    - Year 3: $70,000
- Using a discount factor (simplified to 10% per year):
    - PV Year 1: 50,000 ÷ 1.1 = 45,454
    - PV Year 2: 60,000 ÷ (1.1^2) = 49,587
    - PV Year 3: 70,000 ÷ (1.1^3) = 52,654
- Total present value = 147,695 → approximate business value today

Key Insight: DCF links future potential to today's value. Even small changes in assumptions (growth, risk, discount rate) significantly affect valuation, which is why judgment matters.

Limitations of DCF Models

While DCF is widely used, beginners should understand its limitations:

1. **Forecasting Uncertainty:** Future cash flows are estimates, not guarantees. Unexpected events can significantly alter reality.
    - Example: Market disruption, regulatory changes, or supply chain issues.

2. **Sensitivity to Discount Rates:** Small changes in the rate used to adjust for risk can dramatically change valuation.
   - Example: A 1% change in discount rate can increase or decrease value by tens of thousands of dollars for small companies.
3. **Long-Term Projections:** Predicting cash flows many years into the future is inherently uncertain.
4. **Ignoring Intangibles:** DCF focuses on measurable cash flows and may not fully account for brand value, intellectual property, or human capital.
5. **Complexity in Practice:** While intuitive at a high level, applying DCF to large companies requires careful adjustments for working capital, capital expenditures, and risk factors.

Practical Strategy for Beginners:

- Use DCF as a **framework to think about value**, not a precise number.
- Focus on understanding the **relationship between cash flows, time, and risk**.
- Perform **sensitivity analysis**: check how value changes under different assumptions.

- Complement DCF with **other valuation methods** like comparables or precedent transactions.

Analogy: DCF is like predicting how far a river will flow based on rainfall. It gives a reasonable estimate, but unexpected storms, droughts, or diversions can change the outcome.

Practical Insight: Even at a beginner level, thinking in terms of cash flows rather than accounting profits provides a **clearer, more realistic picture of value**, helping avoid overpaying for a company or misjudging investment potential.

Valuation Using Market Comparisons

Valuation is not just about projecting cash flows. Another common and practical approach is using **market comparisons**, sometimes called **relative valuation**. Instead of trying to predict the future perfectly, this method looks at **how similar companies are valued** and applies those benchmarks to the business in question.

Price-to-Earnings (P/E) Ratio

The **Price-to-Earnings (P/E) ratio** compares a company's market price per share to its earnings per share (EPS).

Formula:

$$\text{P/E Ratio} = \frac{\text{Market Price per Share}}{\text{Earnings per Share (EPS)}}$$

Why it matters:

- It shows how much investors are willing to pay for each dollar of profit.
- A high P/E may indicate **growth expectations**, while a low P/E could signal undervaluation or risk.

Example:

- Company A: Price per share = \$50, EPS = \$5 → P/E = 10
- Company B: Price per share = \$100, EPS = \$10 → P/E = 10

Both companies have the same P/E, meaning the market values them similarly relative to their earnings, even if absolute prices differ.

Practical Insight: P/E works best when comparing companies **in the same industry** with similar growth prospects and risk.

Caution: A very high P/E doesn't always mean "overvalued", it may reflect **strong future growth.** Conversely, a very low P/E doesn't automatically mean a bargain; there could be hidden risks.

Price-to-Sales (P/S) Ratio

The **Price-to-Sales (P/S) ratio** compares a company's market capitalization to its total revenue.

Formula:

$$\text{P/S Ratio} = \frac{\text{Market Cap}}{\text{Annual Sales}}$$

Why it matters:

- Useful for companies that are not yet profitable (EPS might be negative).
- Highlights **how much investors are willing to pay for each dollar of revenue.**

Example:

- Company C has $50 million in revenue and a market cap of $100 million → P/S = 2
- Company D has $20 million in revenue and a market cap of $60 million → P/S = 3

Even though Company D is smaller, investors pay more per sales dollar because they expect higher growth or better margins.

Practical Insight: P/S is especially relevant for **startups or high-growth companies** where earnings may not yet exist but revenue potential drives value.

Using Comparables Correctly

Market comparables are only useful when applied **carefully and contextually**. Beginners often misuse them, leading to misleading conclusions.

Key Considerations:

1. **Industry and business model:** Comparing a software company to a retail chain can be meaningless.

2. **Growth and profitability differences:** High-growth companies usually trade at higher multiples.
3. **Market conditions:** Stock market sentiment and interest rates influence ratios.
4. **Adjust for size and risk:** Smaller companies often carry more risk, which should be reflected in valuation.

Example of Proper Use:

- You want to value a mid-size e-commerce company.
- Find 3–5 publicly traded e-commerce firms of similar size and growth.
- Compare P/E and P/S ratios.
- Apply the **average multiples** to your company's earnings or revenue to estimate a market-based value range.

Example Calculation:

- Target company revenue = $10 million, net profit = $1 million
- Comparable companies P/E average = 15, P/S average = 2
- Market-based valuation using P/E: 1 million × 15 = $15 million

- Market-based valuation using P/S: 10 million × 2 = $20 million
- Estimated value range: $15–20 million

Practical Insight: Comparables provide a **reality check** against cash flow-based intrinsic valuation. If intrinsic value says $18 million and market comparables suggest $15–20 million, you have confidence the estimate is reasonable.

Analogy: Using market comparables is like checking house prices in your neighborhood before selling your own. You combine what your house can earn (or in business terms, cash flow) with what buyers are paying nearby to find a fair price.

Why Valuations Change Over Time

A company's value is not fixed. Even if its cash flows, assets, and operations remain the same, the **perceived value can fluctuate** based on expectations, risk, and market conditions. Understanding why valuations change is crucial for investors, managers, and business owners.

Growth Expectations

Future growth potential is one of the most important drivers of valuation. Investors are willing to pay more for companies that are expected to **grow faster, expand market share, or increase profits consistently**.

Example:

- Company A has stable profits of $1 million per year.
- Company B also has $1 million profits but is expanding into a high-demand market and expected to earn $3 million in three years.
- Investors are likely to value Company B higher because of the **anticipated growth**, even if current profits are identical.

Key Insight: Growth expectations are forward-looking and can cause valuation swings **before actual results are realized.** Over-optimism can inflate value, while unexpected successes can boost it rapidly.

Analogy: Valuing a company based on growth is like buying a tree not for the fruit it currently bears, but for the full harvest it is expected to produce in the future.

Practical Tip: Always distinguish **expected growth** from actual growth. High expectations increase value but also increase risk if targets are missed.

Risk Perception

Risk influences valuation because it affects the **discount rate applied to future cash flows**. Higher perceived risk reduces value, while lower risk increases it.

Factors affecting risk perception:

- **Business risk:** Volatility in sales, competition, or product demand.
- **Financial risk:** Debt levels, cash flow stability, and liquidity.
- **Operational risk:** Dependence on key employees, suppliers, or technology.
- **Regulatory or market risk:** Changes in laws, tariffs, or economic conditions.

Example:

- Two companies have identical cash flows of $1 million next year.
- Company A is in a stable utility sector → low perceived risk → higher valuation.

- Company B is a startup in a volatile market → high perceived risk → lower valuation.

Key Insight: Risk is subjective and dynamic. What investors perceive as risky today may change tomorrow due to new information, management actions, or market events.

Analogy: Risk perception is like insurance. A safer neighborhood has lower premiums, while a flood-prone area increases insurance costs, even if the houses are structurally identical.

Market Sentiment

Market sentiment refers to the **overall mood and behavior of investors**. Even if fundamentals remain strong, valuations can fluctuate based on optimism, fear, or speculation.

Examples of market sentiment impact:

- During a tech boom, investors may pay very high multiples for high-growth companies, inflating value.
- During a market crash, even healthy companies see their market value drop sharply due to fear and uncertainty.

Key Insight: Market sentiment is temporary and can be unpredictable. It can create opportunities for investors who focus on fundamentals rather than hype.

Example:

- Company C has stable earnings and predictable cash flows.
- In a bullish market, its stock may rise 50% above intrinsic value due to excitement about tech trends.
- During a bearish period, the same company may fall 30% below intrinsic value, even though nothing has changed operationally.

Practical Tip: Use market sentiment as a **signal, not a determinant of intrinsic value.** Focus on cash flows, competitive advantages, and realistic growth to anchor valuation decisions.

Key Takeaways

- **Valuations change over time** because of expectations about growth, perceived risk, and market sentiment.
- **Growth expectations** drive value upward but carry the risk of overestimation.

- **Risk perception** directly affects the discounting of future cash flows and valuation.
- **Market sentiment** can temporarily inflate or deflate value, but fundamentals eventually prevail.
- Understanding these factors helps investors and managers make **better-timed decisions**, avoid overpaying, and capitalize on market fluctuations.

Analogy: A company's value is like a kite. Fundamentals are the string holding it steady, but growth expectations, risk, and sentiment act like the wind, pushing it higher or lower.

Practical Insight: Beginners should focus on **intrinsic value** while monitoring market sentiment for opportunities and potential risks. Recognizing why valuations change over time prevents panic or overconfidence and helps make more rational decisions.

Valuation Methods for Beginners

Valuing a business can feel overwhelming, especially for beginners. The numbers, ratios, and models can seem like a secret code only experts understand. The truth is, valuation is much more **intuitive than it appears**. At its core, valuation is about **figuring out what a business is worth based on what it can realistically deliver**, cash, growth, and resilience, while factoring in risk and uncertainty.

This chapter walks you through the most accessible methods for beginners, explains the logic behind them, and shows common pitfalls to avoid.

Cash Flow–Based Valuation Intuition

Cash flow–based valuation, often associated with **discounted cash flow (DCF) methods**, is the most direct way to think about a company's worth. Instead of relying on accounting profits or balance sheet numbers alone, this approach focuses on **the money a business actually generates and can distribute or reinvest**.

The Core Idea:

A business is worth the present value of its **expected future cash flows**. Money today is more valuable than money in the future because of opportunity cost, inflation, and risk.

Intuitive Example:

- Imagine lending $100 to a friend today. In a year, they promise to pay you back $110. That extra $10 is compensation for **time and risk**.
- Similarly, when valuing a company, you are essentially "lending" capital to the business and estimating **what it will pay back over time** in cash.

Why It Matters:

- Cash flow reflects **real liquidity**, not just accounting entries.
- A profitable company can still run into trouble if cash isn't available when needed.
- Cash flow valuation forces you to consider **timing and risk** rather than relying on historical numbers.

Step-by-Step Intuition for Beginners:

1. **Estimate future cash flows:** Think about the company's operations. How much money will it generate after covering costs and investments?
2. **Adjust for risk:** Higher risk reduces value because future cash is less certain.

3. **Bring future cash back to today:** Use a simple discount rate (e.g., 10%) to understand what those future dollars are worth right now.
4. **Sum up the present value:** This gives a realistic range for the company's worth.

Example in Practice:

- Year 1 cash flow: $50,000
- Year 2 cash flow: $60,000
- Year 3 cash flow: $70,000
- Using a 10% discount rate:
    - PV Year 1 = 50,000 ÷ 1.1 = 45,454
    - PV Year 2 = 60,000 ÷ 1.1^2 = 49,587
    - PV Year 3 = 70,000 ÷ 1.1^3 = 52,654
    - Total present value ≈ $147,695

Even at a beginner level, this gives you a **realistic sense of what the business is worth today based on its cash-generating power**.

Practical Insight: Focus on ranges rather than precise numbers. Cash flow estimates are never perfect, but they anchor valuation in reality.

Market Multiples (P/E, Price-to-Sales)

Market multiples provide a **relative valuation approach**. Instead of trying to forecast cash flows in detail, you look at how similar companies are priced in the market and apply those ratios to your company.

Popular Multiples:

- **Price-to-Earnings (P/E) Ratio:** Measures how much investors pay per dollar of profit.
- **Price-to-Sales (P/S) Ratio:** Measures how much investors pay per dollar of revenue, useful when profits are low or negative.

Why Market Multiples Work:

- They reflect what the market is willing to pay for companies with similar growth, profitability, and risk.
- They are simple to apply and **great as a sanity check** against intrinsic valuations like cash flow methods.

Example:

- Your target company earns $2 million in profit, revenue $10 million.
- Similar companies have P/E = 15, P/S = 2.

- Market-based valuation:
    - Using P/E: 2 million × 15 = \$30 million
    - Using P/S: 10 million × 2 = \$20 million
- Estimated range: \$20–30 million

Practical Insight: Market multiples are particularly useful when **cash flows are uncertain**, or you want a quick comparison to industry peers.

Caution: Multiples can be misleading if the company's growth, risk profile, or industry is different from comparables.

When Valuation Methods Fail

No method is perfect. Beginners must understand **why valuation can go wrong.**

Common Scenarios Where Valuation Fails:

1. **Overestimating growth:** Predicting unrealistic revenue or cash flow increases inflates value.
    - Example: A startup promises 50% annual growth for the next five years but operates in a saturated market.
2. **Ignoring risk:** Failing to adjust for volatility, debt levels, or operational challenges leads to overvaluation.

3. **Using wrong comparables:** Comparing a tech startup with a stable retail company can produce meaningless multiples.
4. **Overreliance on accounting numbers:** Focusing only on profits or revenue ignores cash flow realities.
5. **Market bubbles:** High valuations driven by hype rather than fundamentals can mislead investors.

Practical Insight: Always cross-check using **multiple methods** cash flow-based, market multiples, and even simple rules of thumb to get a balanced perspective.

Common Valuation Mistakes

Even seasoned investors can fall into traps. Beginners are particularly vulnerable.

1. **Confusing price with value:** Just because a company trades at $100 per share doesn't mean it is intrinsically worth $100.
2. **Neglecting timing:** A dollar received today is worth more than a dollar received in the future. Ignoring this can overstate value.
3. **Ignoring costs and investments:** Valuing a business based on gross revenue without

considering operational or capital expenses exaggerates worth.

4. **Chasing trends:** Buying into hype without understanding fundamentals can lead to overpayment.
5. **Single-method reliance:** Using only P/E or only DCF can provide a skewed picture. Combining methods reduces risk of misvaluation.

Example of a Mistake:

- A startup reports $500,000 in profit and is growing fast.
- Investors apply a P/E of 50 because tech companies are booming, ignoring that cash flows are inconsistent and debt is high.
- Overvaluation leads to disappointment when results fail to meet inflated expectations.

Practical Tip: Think of valuation as **triangulation**: use multiple methods, check assumptions, and always consider risk.

Bringing It All Together

For beginners, a simple framework is:

1. **Start with cash flow intuition:** Focus on what the business can actually generate.
2. **Use market multiples as a sanity check:** Compare with peers, adjust for differences.
3. **Check assumptions carefully:** Growth rates, discount rates, risk factors, and comparables.
4. **Understand limitations:** Valuation is never exact, treat numbers as **ranges, not absolutes.**
5. **Learn from mistakes:** Analyze past errors to improve judgment over time.

Analogy: Valuation is like predicting the value of a house. You look at:

- **Cash flow analogy:** What rent or income can it generate?
- **Market multiples analogy:** What did similar houses sell for?
- **Assumptions:** Are there upcoming repairs, market changes, or neighborhood trends?
- Combining all gives a **reasonable estimate**, not a guaranteed number.

Key Takeaways

- **Valuation is about estimating what a business is worth based on cash generation, growth, and risk.**

- **Cash flow–based valuation** anchors value in what the company can realistically deliver.
- **Market multiples** provide a relative perspective and reality check against intrinsic value.
- **Valuation methods fail** if assumptions are unrealistic or risks ignored.
- Beginners should **avoid common mistakes** like overreliance on single methods or ignoring timing and cash flows.
- Always **combine approaches**, focus on ranges, and understand that value evolves over time.

Practical Insight: By mastering these beginner-friendly valuation methods, you gain the ability to:

- Assess business opportunities critically
- Avoid overpaying for investments
- Make smarter decisions as a manager, entrepreneur, or investor

Valuation doesn't have to be intimidating. With intuition, careful assumptions, and practical checks, even beginners can **estimate a company's worth confidently and realistically**.

CHAPTER 22

Finance in Everyday Business Decisions

Finance is not just for accountants, CFOs, or big corporations. Every decision a business makes, no matter how small, has financial consequences. Understanding the financial impact of everyday choices empowers managers, entrepreneurs, and employees to make smarter, more profitable decisions.

Finance in daily operations is about **seeing money clearly**, understanding trade-offs, and aligning decisions with business goals. This chapter explores three core areas where finance drives practical decisions: pricing, hiring and expansion, and cash management.

Pricing Decisions and Profit Impact

Pricing is one of the most critical decisions a business makes. It directly affects **revenue, profit, and competitive positioning**. Many beginners assume that price is just what the market will bear, but every price point has financial consequences.

Key Concepts:

- **Revenue vs Profit:** Setting a higher price can increase profit per unit but may reduce sales volume. Conversely, a lower price may boost sales but compress margins.
- **Contribution Margin:** The amount each sale contributes toward covering fixed costs and generating profit. Understanding contribution margin helps in pricing decisions.

Example:

- A bakery sells cupcakes:
    - Cost per cupcake: $1.50
    - Price options: $2.00 or $3.00
- Selling at $2.00 → Profit per cupcake = $0.50
- Selling at $3.00 → Profit per cupcake = $1.50
- But will sales volume drop if the price increases? If sales fall by more than half, total profit may decrease despite higher margins.

Practical Insight: Pricing should balance **profit per unit** and **sales volume**, while considering **market expectations and competitor pricing**.

Analogy: Pricing is like tuning a guitar string: too tight (high price) and it snaps (loses customers); too loose (low price) and it sounds weak (low profit). The right tension hits the sweet spot.

Financial Tip: Track pricing experiments and measure impact on both **revenue and cash flow**. This shows the real financial effect, not just theoretical profit.

Hiring and Expansion as Financial Decisions

Hiring employees or expanding operations is exciting, but every new hire or expansion **commits cash and increases risk**. Treating these as financial decisions ensures sustainability.

Key Considerations:

- **Cost of Hiring:** Salary, benefits, training, and recruitment expenses.
- **Revenue Potential:** Will this hire or expansion generate additional revenue or improve efficiency?
- **Cash Flow Impact:** Even profitable expansion can create cash shortages if timing is not managed.

Example:

- A small retail store wants to hire a new salesperson at $3,000 per month.
- Expected additional monthly sales = $5,000, with gross margin of 50% → $2,500 contribution.
- Financially, this hire **reduces net cash by $500 per month** until sales increase or expenses adjust.

Practical Insight: Every hiring or expansion decision must be evaluated like an investment. If the return (extra revenue or efficiency) does not cover the cost and cash impact, the decision may hurt the business.

Analogy: Hiring is like planting a tree. It takes time to grow (training, adaptation), costs resources (salary, benefits), but eventually provides fruit (revenue and productivity). Plant too many too quickly, and your resources may run dry.

Managing Cash for Survival

Cash management is the backbone of daily business operations. Profit alone does not ensure survival,

without cash on hand, bills go unpaid, suppliers stop delivering, and operations grind to a halt.

Key Principles:

- **Forecast Cash Needs:** Track inflows and outflows daily, weekly, or monthly.
- **Prioritize Payments:** Pay suppliers, employees, and key expenses first.
- **Maintain a Reserve:** A safety cushion helps navigate unexpected slow periods or emergencies.
- **Monitor Timing Gaps:** Understand when revenue is earned vs when cash is collected.

Example:

- A consulting firm bills $50,000 for a project in December but only collects in January.
- Salaries, rent, and supplier bills are due in December → cash shortage occurs despite apparent profit.

Practical Insight: Businesses survive on cash, not profit. Focus on **liquidity, timing, and contingency planning** to avoid crises.

Analogy: Cash is like gasoline in a car. Profit is the engine's power, but without gas, the car won't move. Keeping a steady supply of fuel ensures operations continue smoothly.

Integrating Finance into Everyday Decisions

1. **Think in terms of contribution:** Every decision, pricing, hiring, expansion, should consider its impact on profit contribution and cash flow.
2. **Measure, monitor, adjust:** Track results and adjust decisions based on real financial performance.
3. **Balance risk and reward:** Understand trade-offs; profitable opportunities can fail if cash or resources are insufficient.
4. **Use simple tools:** Even basic spreadsheets or cash flow trackers help visualize the financial impact of daily decisions.

Example:

- A small cafe evaluates two potential menu items:
  - Item A → High margin, low demand
  - Item B → Low margin, high demand

- Using contribution analysis and expected cash flow, the cafe chooses the item that maximizes **overall profitability and liquidity**, not just margin per unit.

Key Takeaways

- **Finance is in every decision.** Pricing, hiring, expansion, and operations all carry financial consequences.
- **Pricing impacts profit and cash flow.** Understanding contribution margins helps find the right balance.
- **Hiring and expansion are investments.** They must cover their costs and positively impact cash flow to be worthwhile.
- **Cash management ensures survival.** Profit is important, but liquidity drives day-to-day operations.
- **Simple financial thinking can prevent costly mistakes.** Even basic awareness of cash, risk, and return improves decision-making.

Practical Insight: Treat every business choice as a financial decision. Even small, everyday decisions accumulate, shaping the company's long-term success or failure. Understanding finance in daily operations turns uncertainty into **informed, strategic action**, helping businesses grow sustainably and avoid crises.

PART VII

APPLYING CORPORATE FINANCE IN REAL LIFE

CHAPTER 23

Thinking Like an Owner, CFO, or Investor

Finance is not just about numbers on a spreadsheet or reports sitting in a binder. It is a **way of thinking**, a lens through which every business decision can be analyzed and understood. Whether you are a business owner, an aspiring CFO, or an investor, learning to think like someone who truly **cares about financial outcomes** is what separates success from costly mistakes.

This chapter focuses on applying financial thinking to **pricing, hiring, expansion, and decision-making**, and it shows how to **build long-term confidence** in interpreting financials.

Finance in Pricing, Hiring, and Expansion Decisions

Every operational decision impacts the bottom line, whether it is **setting a price, hiring a new employee, or expanding operations**. Thinking like an owner means understanding the **trade-offs, risks, and returns** associated with each choice.

Pricing Decisions:

- Pricing is not arbitrary; it determines **profit margins, cash inflow, and market positioning**.
- Owners and investors think beyond sales volume, they consider how each price impacts **contribution margin and sustainability**.
- Example: A software company can sell a subscription for $50/month or $100/month. While $100 maximizes profit per customer, it may reduce adoption. Choosing the right price balances **revenue, growth, and market penetration**.

Hiring Decisions:

- Hiring is an investment. Salaries, benefits, and training costs must be weighed against the expected contribution of the employee.
- Example: A new salesperson costs $3,000/month but is expected to bring in $5,000 in gross margin. Even if profitable, cash timing must be considered to ensure the company can **cover upfront costs without stress**.

Expansion Decisions:

- Expanding to new locations or launching new products requires **capital, operational planning, and risk management**.
- Example: Opening a second store may double potential revenue but also doubles rent, salaries, and inventory needs. CFOs model these cash flows before approving the expansion.

Practical Insight: Owners, CFOs, and investors always ask:

- Will this decision generate more cash than it consumes?
- Does it align with long-term strategic goals?
- What are the risks if things go wrong?

Reading Financials Before Making Decisions

Financial statements are more than numbers, they tell a **story about the business**. Thinking like an investor or CFO requires learning to **interpret these stories** before committing resources.

Income Statement: Shows how profitable operations are. It answers:

- Are we generating enough profit to cover costs and reinvest in growth?
- Which products or services contribute most to profits?

Balance Sheet: Shows what the company owns and owes. Key questions:

- Do we have enough assets to support expansion?
- How leveraged is the company with debt?
- Is there enough equity to absorb unexpected losses?

Cash Flow Statement: Shows the movement of actual cash. Key questions:

- Can we pay employees and suppliers on time?
- Are investments consuming more cash than operations generate?
- Are financing activities sustainable?

Example:

- A company reports $500,000 profit but has a negative cash flow of $50,000.
- A new project may seem profitable on paper, but cash shortages could prevent execution.

- Thinking like a CFO would flag the project until cash flow improves.

Practical Tip: Always **cross-check profit with cash flow and balance sheet strength** before making major business decisions.

Avoiding the Most Costly Beginner Mistakes

Beginners often make financial mistakes that cost far more than necessary. Thinking like an investor or CFO helps **avoid these pitfalls.**

1. **Ignoring cash flow:** Profit is important, but cash keeps the business alive.
2. **Overexpansion:** Growth is tempting, but taking on too many costs or debt can bankrupt a company.
3. **Pricing without margin analysis:** Cutting prices to increase sales can destroy profitability.
4. **Hiring without forecasting:** New hires without clear revenue contribution or cash flow coverage can drain resources.
5. **Neglecting risk assessment:** Every decision carries risk; ignoring it can lead to unexpected financial stress.

Example:

- A cafe hires three new baristas assuming customer growth, but sales stagnate. Cash reserves are depleted, forcing layoffs.
- A small tech startup expands globally without ensuring cash flow, resulting in operational failure despite strong revenue projections.

Lesson: Financial awareness prevents mistakes that appear obvious in hindsight but are easily overlooked by beginners.

Building Long-Term Financial Confidence

Thinking like an owner, CFO, or investor is a skill that **improves with practice**. The goal is to make **confident, informed decisions** rather than reactive or fear-driven ones.

Steps to Build Confidence:

1. **Learn the language of finance:** Understand income statements, balance sheets, and cash flows.
2. **Analyze the numbers, not just the reports:** Look for trends, risks, and opportunities.

3. **Apply finance to decisions:** Treat pricing, hiring, expansion, and investments as financial decisions with measurable outcomes.
4. **Simulate scenarios:** Model "what-if" scenarios to see how decisions affect cash flow, profits, and risk.
5. **Review outcomes:** Compare predicted versus actual results to improve judgment over time.

Analogy: Thinking like a CFO is like driving a car. You don't just look at the speedometer, you watch the road, anticipate curves, and adjust your speed to avoid accidents. Financial reports are your dashboard; decisions are the turns and accelerations.

Practical Insight: The more you integrate financial thinking into everyday business decisions, the less you rely on luck, guesswork, or intuition alone. Over time, this builds **confidence, clarity, and control**.

Key Takeaways

- Every business decision, pricing, hiring, or expansion has financial consequences.
- Thinking like an owner, CFO, or investor means **evaluating cash, profit, risk, and growth simultaneously**.

- Financial statements are tools for decision-making, not just record-keeping.
- Beginners can avoid costly mistakes by focusing on **cash flow, margins, risk, and realistic assumptions**.
- Building financial confidence is a process: learn, apply, analyze, and adjust.
- Integrating finance into everyday thinking ensures decisions are **strategic, informed, and sustainable**.

Practical Advice: Treat every business choice as a financial decision. Ask: Will it generate cash, add value, and manage risk? This mindset turns day-to-day operations into **long-term value creation**, giving you the insight and confidence to grow a business responsibly.

CHAPTER 24

A Simple End-to-End Business Case

Understanding corporate finance in theory is one thing; seeing how it all comes together in a real business scenario is another. This chapter walks you step by step through a **complete business case**, showing how a simple idea translates into financial statements, informs investment decisions, and leads to an estimate of the company's value.

By following this approach, beginners can **connect the dots** between concepts like cash flow, profitability, risk, financing, and valuation in a practical, human way.

From Business Idea to Financial Statements

Every company starts with an idea. The first step is to translate that idea into numbers that describe **how the business will operate and generate money**.

Step 1: Define the Business Idea

- Example: A small bakery plans to sell artisanal cupcakes in a busy city neighborhood.
- Key questions:
    - What products or services will be offered?
    - Who is the target customer?
    - What is the expected demand and sales volume?

Step 2: Estimate Revenue

- Predict how many units will sell per month and at what price.
- Example: 1,000 cupcakes/month × $3 each = $3,000/month revenue.

Step 3: Identify Costs

- Fixed Costs: Rent, salaries, utilities (do not change with sales volume).
    - Example: Rent = $1,000, salaries = $1,500, utilities = $200 → Total fixed = $2,700/month

- Variable Costs: Ingredients, packaging (increase with sales).
  - Example: $1 per cupcake × 1,000 cupcakes = $1,000/month

Step 4: Create an Income Statement

- Revenue: $3,000
- Variable Costs: $1,000
- Contribution Margin: $2,000
- Fixed Costs: $2,700
- Operating Profit: $2,000 – $2,700 = -$700 (loss)

This shows the bakery **needs either higher sales, higher prices, or lower costs** to become profitable.

Step 5: Build a Balance Sheet

- Assets: Oven ($5,000), cash reserves ($1,000), ingredients inventory ($500) → Total $6,500
- Liabilities: Bank loan for oven ($5,000)
- Equity: Owner investment ($1,500)
- Balance Sheet balances: Assets = Liabilities + Equity → $6,500 = $5,000 + $1,500

Step 6: Prepare a Cash Flow Forecast

- Cash Inflows: Sales revenue

- Cash Outflows: Ingredient purchases, salaries, rent, loan repayment
- Example: Even if the bakery shows a small profit, cash may be tight if ingredients are purchased upfront and revenue is collected later.

Practical Insight: Translating an idea into financial statements allows you to **test feasibility before spending large sums of money**.

From Financials to Investment Decisions

Once financial statements are built, they guide **investment and operational decisions**.

Key Areas to Evaluate:

1. **Profitability:**
    - Is the business model capable of generating sustainable profits?
    - In the bakery example, initial analysis shows a loss of $700/month. Decisions may include increasing price, cutting costs, or boosting sales.
2. **Cash Flow:**
    - Can the business cover day-to-day expenses?

    - If cash is tight, the owner might delay hiring, negotiate supplier payments, or secure additional funding.
3. **Break-even Analysis:**
    - How many units need to be sold to cover all costs?
    - Example: Fixed Costs ÷ Contribution Margin per Unit = 2,700 ÷ 2 = 1,350 cupcakes → Need to sell 1,350 cupcakes/month to break even.
4. **Investment Evaluation:**
    - Should the owner invest in a bigger oven for more production?
    - Look at the **expected return on investment (ROI)**, additional cash flow generated, and risk involved.
5. **Risk Consideration:**
    - Assess operational risks: supplier delays, changing demand
    - Financial risks: high debt, insufficient cash reserves

Example Decision:

- The bakery considers a marketing campaign costing $300/month to increase sales by 500 cupcakes/month.

- Additional revenue = 500 × \$3 = \$1,500
- Additional variable cost = 500 × \$1 = \$500
- Contribution from campaign = \$1,000
- Campaign cost = \$300
- Net benefit = \$700 → turns previous \$700 loss into breakeven

This demonstrates **how financial analysis directly informs practical business decisions.**

From Decisions to Valuation

Once the business model, investment decisions, and operational plans are clear, the next step is to estimate the company's value. Beginners can use **simple approaches** without complex formulas.

Step 1: Cash Flow-Based Valuation (Simplified)

- Project cash flows for 3–5 years based on expected sales, costs, and investments.
- Example: After improvements, bakery expected net cash flow: Year 1 = \$1,000, Year 2 = \$2,000, Year 3 = \$3,000
- Estimate present value using a rough discount rate (e.g., 10%):
    - PV Year 1 = 1,000 ÷ 1.1 = 909
    - PV Year 2 = 2,000 ÷ 1.1^2 = 1,653

- PV Year 3 = 3,000 ÷ 1.1^3 = 2,253
- Total PV ≈ $4,815 → approximate value of the bakery

Step 2: Market Multiples (Optional Check)

- Compare to similar businesses: small bakeries sell for 2× annual net cash flow

- Annual cash flow Year 3 = $3,000 × 12 = $36,000

- Estimated value using multiples = $36,000 × 2 = $72,000

- Observation: Multiples often give a higher "market perception" value, while cash flow valuation is more conservative. Both methods combined provide a **range of reasonable values.**

Step 3: Consider Growth and Risk

- Growth potential: Can the bakery open additional stores? Offer catering? Expand products?
- Risk factors: Seasonal demand, competition, or rising ingredient costs

- Adjust valuation accordingly → a higher-risk, lower-growth scenario reduces value; strong growth prospects increase value.

Step 4: Make Final Decisions

- If the estimated value is higher than the cost of buying or starting the bakery, it's a potentially **good investment.**
- Decisions on expansion, financing, or pricing can now be **tested against their effect on valuation**, not just immediate profit.

Practical Insight: Thinking in terms of cash flow, risk, and market comparisons allows beginners to see **how every decision from a marketing campaign to a new hire affects the overall value of the business.**

Conclusion

Key Lessons and Next Steps

After working through a complete business case from idea to financial statements, investment decisions, and valuation, the final step is to **internalize the lessons and develop habits that make you a smarter decision-maker.** This section distills the core principles, shows how to keep improving your financial judgment, and helps you apply corporate finance with confidence in real-world situations.

Core Principles Every Reader Should Remember

Throughout this book, certain **foundational truths** about corporate finance keep resurfacing. These are the principles that separate businesses that survive and grow from those that struggle or fail.

1. Profit is important, but cash is critical.

- A business can show profits on paper but still fail if it cannot pay employees, suppliers, or creditors.
- Always evaluate cash flow alongside profit to see the true financial health of a company.

2. Every decision has a financial impact.

- Pricing, hiring, expansion, and even small operational choices affect revenue, costs, and cash.
- Thinking like an owner, CFO, or investor means weighing trade-offs and considering both short-term and long-term consequences.

3. Risk matters as much as return.

- No investment is guaranteed. High potential returns often come with high risk.
- Understanding both business and financial risk allows you to make better, more informed decisions.

4. Numbers tell a story, but context matters.

- Financial statements are tools, not absolute truths. They must be interpreted carefully in light of strategy, market conditions, and operational realities.

5. Valuation is an art guided by science.

- Business value is based on expected cash flows, growth, and risk.
- Understanding valuation helps prioritize investments, compare opportunities, and make decisions grounded in reality rather than intuition alone.

6. Learning and judgment improve with practice.

- Finance is a skill you build over time. Real understanding comes from **applying concepts, reviewing results, and adjusting strategies**.

How to Keep Improving Financial Judgment

Becoming confident in corporate finance is not a one-time achievement. It is an **ongoing process of learning and application.**

1. Review Financial Statements Regularly

- Analyze income statements, balance sheets, and cash flow statements monthly.
- Compare actual results with forecasts to see where expectations match reality.

2. Apply Concepts to Real Decisions

- Treat even small business decisions, like pricing a product or hiring a contractor, as financial exercises.
- Estimate cash flows, assess risk, and forecast outcomes before acting.

3. Learn From Mistakes and Successes

- Every financial misstep or success is a lesson.
- Document decisions and outcomes. Over time, patterns emerge that improve judgment.

4. Use Simple Tools

- Spreadsheets, cash flow trackers, and financial dashboards make analysis manageable.
- Visualizing data clarifies trends, risks, and opportunities.

5. Stay Curious About Business Performance

- Ask questions: Why did sales rise? Why did cash flow dip? How did a competitor succeed?
- Curiosity strengthens your ability to interpret numbers and anticipate challenges.

6. Seek Mentorship or Guidance

- Learning from experienced managers, CFOs, or investors accelerates your understanding.
- Observing how they make decisions provides practical insights beyond textbooks.

Applying Corporate Finance With Confidence

The ultimate goal is to **translate knowledge into action**. Confidence comes from seeing how the pieces, financial statements, ratios, cash flow, investments, and valuation, fit together in practical business scenarios.

Steps to Apply Finance Confidently:

1. Frame Every Decision Financially

- Before acting, ask: How does this affect cash, profit, risk, and value?

2. Focus on Key Drivers

- Identify the few metrics that really determine business success: cash flow, margins, revenue growth, and risk exposure.

3. Make Trade-offs Explicit

- Recognize that no decision is perfect. Trade-offs are inevitable. Evaluating options clearly helps prioritize wisely.

4. Use Simple Forecasts

- Even basic cash flow projections or break-even calculations are better than guessing.
- Forecast the short-term and long-term financial impact before committing resources.

5. Learn to Step Back

- Avoid getting lost in daily operations. Periodically review the big picture: overall profitability, cash position, and business value.

6. Develop a Repeatable Process

- Collect data → Analyze → Decide → Review outcomes → Adjust
- Over time, this process builds financial intuition that rivals formal education.

7. Embrace Continuous Learning

- Business and markets change. Keep updating your knowledge of financial concepts, valuation techniques, and industry trends.

Example in Practice:

Imagine you own a small retail business and are considering adding a new product line:

- **Step 1:** Estimate revenue and contribution margin per unit.
- **Step 2:** Assess required investment in inventory, marketing, and staffing.
- **Step 3:** Project cash flow impact over the first 6–12 months.

- **Step 4:** Evaluate risk: How sensitive is cash flow to sales fluctuations?
- **Step 5:** Decide based on whether the expected return justifies the risk and aligns with strategic goals.

Following this approach, every decision is grounded in numbers, risk assessment, and strategic thinking, just like a CFO or investor would.

Key Takeaways

- **Finance is a mindset.** Thinking like an owner, CFO, or investor transforms decisions into strategic actions.
- **Review, analyze, and forecast.** Regular engagement with financial statements builds confidence and skill.
- **Avoid common mistakes.** Focus on cash, margins, risk, and long-term value to prevent costly errors.
- **Decisions should be measured, deliberate, and repeatable.** Use simple forecasts, contribution analysis, and scenario thinking.
- **Continuous learning is critical.** Markets, costs, and business models evolve; financial judgment grows with experience.

- **Integrating finance into everyday decisions empowers action.** Even small businesses can make smarter choices and maximize value with disciplined financial thinking.

Practical Insight: Corporate finance is not reserved for accountants or CFOs. By internalizing these principles, **any entrepreneur, manager, or professional can make confident, informed, and profitable decisions**, turning theory into real-world results.

www.ingramcontent.com/pod-product-compliance
Lightning Source LLC
LaVergne TN
LVHW052305200926
848481LV00002B/465
* 9 7 9 8 2 9 5 6 5 2 9 3 6 *